The Law is an Ass

At 35, Gyles Brandreth – the son and grandson of lawyers – is a former Oxford Scholar, President of the Oxford Union, Artistic Director of the Oxford Theatre Festival, founder of the British Pantomime Association, Organizer of the National Scrabble Championships, European Monopoly Champion and holder of the world record for the longest-ever after-dinner speech – 12½ hours! He has written for a dozen national newspapers and magazines and his weekly Alphabet Soup column is syndicated throughout the United States. He has made over a thousand appearances on radio and television and sold more than ten million copies of his many books.

Gyles Brandreth

The Law is an Ass

with cartoons by Tony Matthews

Pan Original
Pan Books London and Sydney

First published 1984 by Pan Books Ltd,
Cavaye Place, London SW10 9PG
© Gyles Brandreth 1984
ISBN 0 330 28210 7

Photoset by Parker Typesetting Service, Leicester
Printed and bound in Great Britain by
Collins, Glasgow

Contents

'If the law supposes that,' said Mr Bumble . . . 'the law is a ass — a idiot.'
Charles Dickens, 'Oliver Twist'

Introduction

Once upon a time – in 1864 to be exact – in the tiny country of Andorra, the government issued this historic decree:

> The appearance in our courts of the learned gentlemen of the law, who can make black appear white and white appear black, is forbidden.

The decree is still in force and to this day Andorra boasts only one lawyer – who never goes to court. He sits quietly in his office, drafting wills, sharpening pencils and conveyancing property.

In no other country on earth are there so few lawyers so innocuously employed. According to the best guestimate I have come across – in the *New York Times* in 1983 – in the Western world as a whole, over five million people (the equivalent of the entire population of Denmark) are engaged in some aspect of the law and law enforcement. And, if you believed everything you ever read in a dictionary of quotations you'd come to the conclusion that most of them are thoroughly unpopular and deserve to be:

> You're a lawyer. It's your duty to lie, conceal and distort everything, and slander everybody.
> Jean Giraudoux

A man may as well open an oyster without a knife, as a lawyer's
mouth without a fee.

Barten Holyday

The minute you read something you can't understand, you can
almost be sure it was drawn up by a lawyer.

Will Rogers

In my time I have had considerable dealings with the law. I have
been a litigant ('Litigant: a person about to give up his skin for
the hope of retaining his bones' – Ambrose Bierce), a juror ('A
jury consists of twelve persons chosen to decide who has the
better lawyer' – Robert Frost) and a courtroom reporter ('Courtroom: A place where Jesus Christ and Judas Iscariot would be
equals, with the betting odds in favour of Judas' – H. L. Men-
cken).

Despite skirmishes with several traffic wardens, two policemen
and H. M. Commissioner of Customs and Excise, I am, as a rule,
an upholder of the law (if inclined to endorse Mae West's
maxim: 'It ain't no sin if you crack a few laws now and then, just
so long as you don't break any'), and I reckon I'm well advised
since the law tends to have might (if not always right) on its side.
(A young Oxford don once proposed the motion to Dr Ben-
jamin Jowett, the great Victorian Master of Balliol, that *priests*
were far more important than *judges*.

Said the don: 'A judge can only say "You be hanged", but a
priest can say "You be damned".'

Answered Jowett: 'Yes, but if a judge says "You be hanged",
you *are* hanged.')

I am the grandson of a solicitor and the son of a barrister, a
solicitor and a magistrate (no, I don't have three parents: my
father had a go at each in his time) and I have to confess that
some of my best friends are lawyers. This book is really their
work, not mine. It is a collection of all the true stories I've ever
heard about the law in all its aspects – from ridiculous laws to
ridiculous lawyers, from artful criminals to eccentric testators,
from wayward witnesses to razor-edged attorneys, from pedes-
trian prosecutors to prosecuted pedestrians, from ignorance in
the dock to insobriety on the bench. All human life is here.

Are all policemen stupid? Is every judge a reactionary dotard? Has there ever been a lawyer who wasn't an avaricious crook at heart? *Is the law an ass?* Here is the evidence. For once it is up to you to bring in the verdict.

All in the line of duty

A police sergeant who discovered that the licence on his mongrel terrier had expired wasted no time in taking the appropriate action. 'My very first act was to take out a summons against myself,' he told the court hearing his case.

In an effort to improve relations between the people of Dorset and their police force, the Assistant Chief Constable told his officers, 'Mingle with the community – especially at parties. I want the people to realize the police are human. We want the men to visit parties, take their helmets off and have a cup of tea and a sticky bun.'

Public relations were clearly foremost in the mind of an Irish police press officer who brushed off murmurs of concern at the escape from police custody of a murder suspect with the reassuring remark, 'He is no more dangerous than any other murderer.'

A speaker at a law and order seminar told his audience that prejudice was a necessary ingredient in any policeman concerned with doing his job properly. 'Prejudice is a state of mind brought about by experience,' he explained.

Many officers are concerned about the image of the force to such an extent that it was reported some time ago that detectives in Sheffield did not carry notebooks because they spoiled the fit of their jackets.

The problems raised by the struggle against pornography have been around for far longer than current reports might lead us to believe. Thirty years ago Scotland Yard was on the look-out for new premises in which to store the huge stock of obscene material it had already amassed. The Customs who had impounded the books and magazines were all for putting a match to the pile but the material was unfortunately stored within a smokeless zone which ruled out the most obvious solution.

'Simple and traditional' police methods were advocated by one of the Chiefs of the Los Angeles Police who drew up plans for a mobile gallows to deal swiftly and surely with hijackers. 'We have a moving courtroom in a bus and the gallows is towed behind it in a small trailer,' he told reporters when the plans were unveiled. 'As soon as the criminal is grabbed, we hold a quick trial, find him guilty, and hang him on the main runway right beneath the observation platform. My gallows has a titanium crossbar and a nylon rope – the trap is fully automatic. All I am waiting for is the reintroduction of the death penalty.'

An even more unorthodox line of duty was taken by four Egyptian policemen detailed to escort a coffin to a Cairo cemetery. According to statements made later, the four of them had felt an irresistible power coming from inside the coffin which forced them to deviate from their set route and drive instead to the racecourse. There the force indicated which horses they should back and from the stands they had the satisfaction of watching them all win. The matter might never have come to light had not members of the public become alarmed at the sight of the coffin standing among them beside its police bodyguard.

The dividing line between a policeman's duty to the public and his respect for the law of the land can be alarmingly narrow at times. One constable who had been booked by a fellow officer for parking illegally explained his predicament to the magistrates, saying, 'I had to attend this court as a witness. I knew that twenty minutes is the parking limit without special permission from a uniformed policeman. I was in uniform and there was no other policeman in sight then, so I gave myself permission.'

A motorist in Atlanta, Georgia, returned to his parked car, turned the ignition key to drive off and discovered that the engine wouldn't turn over. This fault was soon explained when he found that the battery had been stolen and the fuel tank drained. He walked to a nearby garage to buy another battery and more fuel and returned to find that the two front wheels had been pinched. He went off in search of two replacements but when he returned with these he discovered that the whole car had vanished. His next visit was to the police station to report the loss. Here he met with greater success. A passing patrolman had seen the partly stripped car by the side of the road and, assuming that it had been abandoned, made arrangements for it to be hauled away.

An Irish policeman who thought he heard a bomb explode went to investigate and found that the cause of the noise was a seventeen-year-old Mini driving along at a brisk walking pace. The officer asked the driver to stop and started to examine his vehicle. He explained afterwards, 'I found that it would not engage in any gear but first, had four completely bald tyres, neither hand nor foot brake worked, the steering was marshy, the battery flat, the spare tyre deflated, three hub-caps missing, the car had no driving mirror and was covered in mud. While I was making an examination the exhaust pipe fell off and the engine boiled.' The driver, who had bought the car 'from a passer-by' for £6, told the officer that he had been forced to drive the car in its condition and without insurance when he failed to get a lift to hospital after breaking a leg trying to jack up the car.

Pedestrians in Catford were alarmed to see a driverless car hurtling towards them down Northwood Road, mount the pavement and crash into the rear of a parked van. Not that they would have derived much comfort from knowing that there was in fact a driver in the car, had they heard her explanation to the police: 'I bent down to pick something off the floor of the car. My handbag, five library books and some flower pots had slid on to the floor.'

A Perivale woman stopped by a patrol car for driving unaccompanied and with no 'L' plates while still a learner, was adamant that she was not alone. 'The invisible man was driving my car,' she said, 'and I know that was Christ who guided me. He was sitting in the car with me and supervising my driving . . . I am a Christian and I know I have not done wrong.'

A driver in South Devon was stopped by one of the county's policeman and charged with failing to have proper control of his vehicle. The officer wasn't concerned with whether the driver had been drinking or not, his worry was one of the passengers. 'As the vehicle drew near I saw the backside and tail of a donkey through the windscreen and very close to the driver,' he told the court hearing the case. 'On causing the defendant to stop, I confirmed that the animal was a donkey.' Further investigation revealed that all the seats but the driver's had been removed and that his wife was sitting on the floor in the back holding the animal's halter. All this, claimed the prosecution, confirmed that the driver did not have adequate vision with which to drive safely.

In his defence the driver maintained that the donkey was very tame. He also produced a photograph showing that he had been able to see along either side of the car and even between the donkey's back and the car's roof. In the face of this evidence the case was dismissed.

A Californian motorist, stopped by a highway patrol after driving straight through a red traffic light, told the officer with impeccable logic, 'If I make any sudden moves my wife spills her breakfast and that makes her mad.' This statement was confirmed by the lady sitting beside the driver consuming a plateful of bacon and eggs.

The sight of a naked woman leaning out of the window of a passing car and waving for help prompted a traffic officer in north Oxfordshire to give chase and stop the offending driver. Closer inspection revealed that the 'lady' was in fact a life-size inflatable doll 'with breasts and other convincing attributes'. She had been a present from friends, the driver explained. His wife had just deserted him and the doll was their way of trying to cheer him up. 'After a few drinks I took a liking to the doll,' he said, 'and decided to take her for a spin in the country.' The officer was not convinced and neither, it seemed, were the magistrates, who fined him £25 for carrying a dangerous load.

Patrolling down the M1 late one evening, a police car noticed a Rolls Royce parked on the hard shoulder and the figure of a man spending a penny at the side. The policeman stopped and asked the man what he was doing. He replied that he thought the answer was pretty obvious. He had been taken short between service areas and since there was virtually no traffic on the road had taken a chance and relieved himself at the verge. He was asked if he had been drinking and when he replied that he had, out came the breathalyser which showed a very positive reading. While one of the officers drove off to headquarters, the other said he would take the Rolls and its owner, since the man was obviously in no fit state to drive. Only when his colleague had left in the patrol car and he had walked up to the driver's door did he see the chauffeur who had been waiting patiently for his boss to return to the car before continuing their journey!

When a Durham police car was forced to the side of the road by a car belonging to a Chester-le-Street baker the policemen inside quickly apprehended the owner and asked him to take a breath test. He refused. Following their regulations, they then took him to the police station where a doctor asked if he would agree to give a blood sample. Yes, said the baker, provided the sample came from his big toe. There was a risk of infection there, the doctor told him, and for that reason the conventional sites were the ear, thumb or arm. But the baker stuck by his toe and no blood sample was taken.

When the case came to court the defence argued, 'There would be a risk of infection wherever the sample was taken. It is not laid down anywhere in the Act that a person must give a blood sample from any particular place on his body.' In addition counsel submitted that the prosecution had produced no evidence that the baker had even been driving the car when the incident occurred. The case was dismissed.

In 1971 the drug squad in Marseilles took delivery of a new weapon in their crackdown on the growing drug traffic. A camper-van fitted with sophisticated sniffing-gear and a roof-mounted snorkel patrolled the city like a television detector van, smelling out the acetic anhydrides used in the manufacture of heroin. The initial results were impressive, though when police investigated all the sites of positive readings, their enthusiasm waned. The detectors had pin-pointed every restaurant in the city, not in response to illicit heroin, but to the more ubiquitous salad cream.

In the summer of 1797, when England was at war with France and the country was alive with rumours of a pending French invasion, Detective Walsh, stationed in Somerset, received a note from an informer which read, 'The man (with a woman who passes for his sister) has Camp Stools, which he and his visitors take with them when they go about the country upon their nocturnal or diurnal excursions. They also have a portfolio in which they enter their observations, which they have been heard to say were almost finished.'

Working on this tip Walsh shadowed the mysterious couple and the man who frequently accompanied them. Hiding himself, sometimes for hours on end, he listened to their conversations, and for weeks patiently trailed them as they walked across the Quantock hills without once stumbling across the truth. The 'man' referred to by the informer was William Wordsworth, the woman was indeed his sister, Dorothy, and their companion was known locally as Samuel Coleridge.

Crime prevention in Hampstead faced an uphill battle, said the officer responsible a few years ago. Commenting on the alarming increase in car thefts he told reporters, 'The trouble with Hampstead people is that they don't seem to worry if a thing is stolen. They just go out and buy a replacement.'

A Scottish police inspector posing as a black-marketeer nabbed a couple of would-be customers who had been trying to buy the gold he claimed to be offering for sale. His success was short-lived when the two prisoners admitted that they were also undercover policemen masquerading as illegal bullion dealers.

When a shoplifting case came before magistrates at Heanor, Derbyshire, the officer in charge of the case had to apologize to the court for the absence of the vital prosecution exhibit, a minced-beef pie which, he disclosed, had been eaten by mistake.

If police still work on the principle that criminals return to the scenes of their crimes, they don't appear to have cottoned on to the unlikely possibility that they might also put in an appearance at the courtroom, before being obliged to appear in the dock themselves, that is. Yet after an escaped prisoner did a bunk, this is exactly what he did. In the meantime 6,000 police officers spent eight frustrating weeks trying to track him down, all to no avail. When he was eventually apprehended, he was found in the public gallery at Bradford Magistrates Court, dressed as a woman and holding a two-year-old girl on his lap. Safely in police custody again, he said that he had gone to the court to hear the case of his grandmother who was answering a charge of drunken driving.

Following complaints that drunks were lying in the street, police in York took half a dozen French dancing girls to their station for questioning. They were later released with full apologies when it became clear that the girls, members of the Danse Théâtre de Paris, had actually been staging spontaneous performances to advertise their event at the York Festival.

Magistrates at Thames Court heard from a police constable how he had arrested a suspect believing him to be drunk. 'He was unsteady on his feet,' said the officer, 'his breath smelt of alcohol and his eyes were glazed.'

'It was bound to be glazed,' retorted the witness who removed his artificial right eye to prove the point.

'The other one was glazed too,' countered the policeman desperately, but his case had been undermined and the defendant was discharged for three months.

A tip-off from a man who had recently had his watch stolen led Thai police to a deserted hut in a village near Bangkok one night. Their informant had mentioned that among those with whom he would be playing cards in the hut was a thief, the man who had stolen the watch, who had been on the wanted list for several months. He even sent a photograph to help them identify their man. When they raided the hut, however, it was the informant who was shot. Having apologized to his family a police spokesman explained that the informant had accidentally enclosed a picture of himself rather than that of the criminal.

On a similar note comes the story of a detective in Gloucestershire, who approached the manager of a café to ask if he could use his premises to keep watch on suspicious activity in the street outside. The manager took a close look at the officer's photograph on his warrant card and returned it saying, 'I'm sorry, I have never seen that man in here.'

In the days before portable police radios a sergeant on duty in West London arrested two men and then tried to summon help. Presumably his whistle was of little use and he resorted to dialling 999, which didn't get him any further. In the end he had to borrow twopence from one of the suspects in order to ring his station.

A London Transport passenger making a phone call late one night from a coin box in Cannon Street underground station found himself trapped when he was plunged into darkness and discovered all the gates locked. Groping back to the phone he managed to dial 999 and explained his predicament. 'That number is for life-and-death,' the operator told him. Dial 0.' The man dialled 0 and got through to the same operator, who contacted the police.

Police in Ocean Beach, New York, arrested three men and charged them with eating in public, according to the town's anti-litter laws that also ban the carrying of open containers of food. One defendant had been caught red-handed eating a chocolate biscuit, another was eating crumb cake and the third had been seen with a glass of water. When they complained that people were walking about eating ice-creams with impunity the trio were told that that was a long-standing privilege protected by the law.

Police in Southampton were puzzled by the strange case of a sailor who had to be taken to hospital with a two-inch nail sticking out of his skull. The victim told them that he had been having a drink in a Southampton pub when he felt a migraine attack coming on. 'It felt as if I had a bubble in my head ready to burst and so I asked the chaps with me to bang a nail through my skull. They agreed,' he added. 'After that the headache completely disappeared, and I felt better altogether.'

A witness told police, 'He was a stranger to me. He told me he had found a cure for headaches and showed me the top of a nail sticking out of his skull. He said it had happened two hours before at a party.' The woman accompanied the sailor to hospital where the nail was removed.

'There is no question of black magic being involved in any way,' a police spokesman said later. 'We are still continuing our investigations. But the man is completely happy about the whole affair, says that he does not know the name of the person who banged the nail in his head, and wants no action taken.'

After South Carolina police raided one of the state's most notorious brothels and arrested 800 clients found there, the station was bombarded with phone calls from men desperately trying to have their names removed from the charge sheet. There was one lone caller who phoned with a different request, though. This was an elderly man who offered a hundred dollars to have his name added to the list of the accused.

In answer to an emergency call police in Corpus Christi, Texas, arrived at the caller's house and found an irate housewife who insisted that they arrest her husband who was sitting inside, drunk. They tactfully pointed out that there was nothing preventing a man from being drunk in his own home, but this didn't satisfy the wife. She dragged her husband outside into the street, where the police were then able to arrest him.

A sad case dating from the end of the eighteenth century provides a sobering lesson on the dangers of relying too heavily on circumstantial evidence. This concerned a man found guilty at one of the provincial assizes of murdering his niece. As one account states, 'The circumstances sworn to were as follows: That the uncle and the niece were seen walking in the fields; that a person at a small distance heard the niece exclaim, 'Don't kill me, Uncle! Don't kill me!' — and at that instant a pistol or fowling-piece was fired off. Upon these circumstances the gentleman was convicted and executed. Nearly twelve months after, the niece who had eloped, arrived in England, and hearing of the affair, elucidated the whole incident. It appeared that she had formed an attachment for a person of whom her uncle disapproved: when walking in the fields, he was earnestly dissuading her from the connection, whereupon she replied that she was resolved to have him, or it would be her death. She therefore said, 'Don't kill me, Uncle! Don't kill me!'

At the moment she uttered these words a fowling-piece was discharged by a sportsman in a neighbouring field. The same night she eloped from her uncle's house, and the combination of these suspicious circumstances, occasioned his ignominious death.

A chance combination of circumstances of a very different sort brought about an unexpected interruption in a football game between a team from Hoylake and the Liverpool Police side. A bare five minutes after the start of the second half one of the Hoylake forwards was arrested on the field, which brought cries of disapproval from the Hoylake faction. After the game a police spokesman commented that the facts that the police were losing and that the arrested man had scored several of the goals against them had no bearing on his departure from the game. For his own part the defendant acknowledged that his arrest had been due to the late payment of a fine. 'Several matters became intertwined,' added the policeman.

A young chef stepping off a train in Shoreham, Sussex, found himself surrounded by four policemen. 'Hand it over,' said one of them indicating a bulge in the chef's jacket. The suspect fumbled inside and brought out a fish, saying, 'I bought it for my cat. I was in a hurry and stuffed it inside my jacket.' The officers thanked him for helping them and allowed him on his way. It was later admitted that they had been working on a tip-off that a man carrying a gun in a shoulder-holster had been seen on the train.

The charge of 'assaulting a police officer and wilfully damaging the constable's upper dentures', was made against a man who appeared in front of magistrates at Greenwich. After hearing evidence from both sides, the magistrates were doubtful about the prosecution claim. The accused had admitted cutting the policeman in the mouth, they acknowledged, but they failed to understand how he could have known that the officer was wearing dentures. And, if he did not know about the dentures, how could he have wilfully damaged them, they asked.

A Yarmouth man, who took a fancy to a sheepskin coat in the lobby of a Bognor Regis hotel and made off with it, ran out of luck when he hitched a lift from a passing coach. To his dismay he found it filled with forty detective chief inspectors returning from a crime seminar. Worse was to come. He'd only been on the coach a couple of minutes when one of the passengers took a close interest in the coat he was wearing and after feeling the collar told the man it was his own. 'I realized that I had made a terrible mistake,' admitted the thief later after the coach had delivered him to the nearest police station.

Since the increase of bomb explosions in recent years, police forces have had to deal with countless hoax calls and through necessity they have become accustomed to checking each call carefully. This was certainly the case when a caller with an Irish accent rang the Greater Manchester police to tell them about a bomb planted in one of the city's largest department stores. The duty officer who took the call, suspected that it might be a hoax and didn't treat it with the degree of flustered panic that the caller had expected. In fact he was so annoyed at the policeman's matter-of-fact approach that he said he was going to complain about his behaviour. The officer accordingly asked for his name so that his complaint could be passed on, and the caller gladly gave it!

When Scottish police asked the proprietor of a Chinese restaurant to attend an identity parade, they didn't expect him to turn up dressed as a lion. However, the man told the officer in charge that he was so terrified of a Triad terror group, the Soi Fang, that he had gone in disguise so that no one would recognize him.

Early on the morning of New Year's Day police in Ryde, Isle of Wight, noticed a struggle going on between two men inside the window of a men's outfitters. As a result of this a Scotsman was arrested and charged with shop-breaking. When his case came to court, the accused told the magistrates, 'I heard a crash of glass from the shop. I saw two men running away and spotted what I thought was another man in the window. I crawled through a hole in the glass and leapt on him.' It was only at that stage that he realized that he'd just taken on a tailor's dummy, and it was in this state that the police found him. The magistrates agreed that he had acted from public spirit more than dishonesty and discharged him.

Police in Brittany arrested a number of nudists on Lorient Beach and charged them with breaking the local by-law that forbids nudism. Among those apprehended was one man who stubbornly insisted that, in spite of appearances, he was not a nudist. 'I am not a nudist,' he maintained. 'I am a member of "Decency", an anti-nudist group. I had been sent to the nudist colony as a spy.'

It turned out, however, that the police had their own spies as well, and these had observed the fifth-columnist paying more than passing attention to a group of comely female nudists at the spot where he was arrested. 'I was just asking my way off the beach,' he insisted, but the police didn't believe him any more than the girls had.

When sparking plugs started disappearing from a factory in Denver, Colorado, the management took steps to catch the thief and eventually called in the police to help. The number of suspects was soon narrowed down and when the culprit was caught, 290,000 sparking plugs were found stacked in his house. 'I just like to see them around,' he said in his statement.

Pleading guilty to stealing one hundredweight of liquid chocolate, a thief told police that he had decided to patch things up with his wife who had just been awarded a separation order. She liked chocolate, so he had decided to give her a present.

Banking hours, as many customers have had reason to comment, are not the most convenient for people with 9-to-5 jobs, but East Kent police who found an unemployed labourer prowling inside the bank in Cliftonville late one October evening, suspected his motives when he told them, 'I've come about my overdraft.'

Derbyshire police who arrested a man on a charge of attempted murder after he had bought a knife in Chesterfield and taken it to the victim's house, were told by their prisoner, 'I didn't really attempt to murder her, I really wanted to frighten her to death.'

When Glasgow police arrested a man who had attacked his wife with an axe, the prisoner was unrepentant. 'I should have killed her and got it done with,' he said when cautioned, adding, 'Anyway, did you hear how Celtic got on?'

A bid to rescue two fellow countrymen resulted in an unexpected act of philanthropy when retired US Colonel Arthur 'Bull' Simons broke into Gasre prison, Tehran in February 1979. The colonel had intended freeing two American prisoners but 11,000 others took advantage of his gesture and made their own getaway in the early days of the Iranian revolution.

Not every prisoner is hellbent on getting out of gaol, or so it would appear from the alarming report that Scotland Yard had discovered prisoners in Brixton Prison who were taking it in turns to nip over the wall for a drink or two before returning to their cells. Hard evidence of this breach of the rules was provided by one inmate who was arrested early one morning outside one of the prison walls which he had been trying to scale, in order to get back inside.

When he refused to pay for the breakfast he had just consumed in a Birmingham café, an 86-year-old pensioner was arrested and later put in prison for the night. The following day the authorities agreed to his release, but the old man refused to budge. 'Anyone who has to struggle along on a pension would be mad to leave Winson Green prison,' he explained. 'It's a real treat. Three square meals a day, central heating and plenty of new faces.'

The long and short of it was that the old boy remained behind bars for three months, constantly refusing to be let out. In the end he was forced to leave by the prosecution who applied for bail on his behalf.

'I was hoping to stay in for Christmas,' said the disappointed prisoner. 'They say it's very, very good. Unfortunately I'll just have to find a room somewhere.'

His spell in Winson Green had cost the best part of £400. The cost of the disputed breakfast had been 47p!

Perhaps the problems faced by all law enforcers in striking a balance between these conflicting demands of liberalism and severity should be left to a former Governor of New York State, Al Smith, who spoke to the inmates of Sing Sing prison only a short time after his election to office.

It wasn't until he got to his feet that Smith realized he didn't know how to address his audience. He started with 'My fellow citizens', but quickly dropped that, remembering that they'd forfeited their rights of citizenship when they were put behind bars. Next came, 'My fellow convicts', but that, too, presented problems. With sounds of restlessness coming from the hall, Smith ditched the customary greetings and launched into his speech with the opening sentence, 'Well, in any case – I'm glad to see so many of you here . . .'

With a command of oratory like that it seems surprising that he was beaten to the Democratic nomination in 1928.

As the recruiting advertisements tell us there is nothing routine about the role of the police. More to the point the man on the beat has to be ready to face any eventuality. Two Oban constables patrolling the town at one o'clock one morning when they came across two men trying to tie a 4½-foot basking shark to a lamp-post. They ordered them to undo their gear, which consisted of a grappling hook tied to a length of rope, and told them to take the fish to the police station where the matter could be dealt with in an orderly manner.

For true aplomb it's hard to beat the Assistant Chief Constable of the West Yorkshire force, George Oldfield, who was asked during the long search for the mass murderer in his region, then styling himself as 'Jack the Ripper', whether he was going to call in Scotland Yard; he replied, 'Why should I? They haven't caught theirs yet.'

'For the middle class, the police protect property, give directions and help old ladies. For the urban poor, the police are those who arrest you,' said Michael Harrington, and attitudes towards the police clearly depend on the eyes of the beholder. Yet to many people the regulations governing police work are themselves anachronistic and unbending. The new police headquarters and courthouse opened in East Grinstead some twenty years ago had lavatories marked 'Ladies' and 'Gentlemen' for the magistrates; 'Men' and 'Women' for members of the public; and 'Male' and 'Female' for the staff.

Let justice be done

Being a judge is the best career in the world. One is never contradicted, one is never interrupted, and one always has the last word.

Mr Justice Vaisey

When a former Lord Chief Justice was asked to sum up his work he told the questioner, 'The greater part of my official time is spent on investigating collisions between propelled vehicles, each on its own side of the road, each sounding its horn, and each stationary.' The work of the judge or magistrate is never easy; at least it isn't today. In the past there were those notorious figures on the bench, the hanging judges, like Lord Braxfield who relished the opportunity of sending his victims to the gallows with the wry remark that 'he would be nane the waur of a hangin''. (This was the judge who when reminded that Christ had himself been something of a social reformer, replied, 'Weel, he was hangit.') 'Hang a thief when he's young and he'll no' steal when he's old' was another of his favourite maxims and during the political crises of 1793 he was frequently heard commenting, 'Let them bring me prisoners and I'll find them law.'

Since the abolition of capital punishment judges have lost their ultimate sanction, not that this has diminished their status, nor the awe with which they are viewed by the public. As Judge H. C. Leon commented a few years ago, 'I think that a judge should be looked on rather as a sphinx than as a person – you shouldn't be able to imagine a judge having a bath.' His ideas were startlingly reflected in the mien of Mr Justice Avory, known as 'The Acid

Drop' for his singular lack of humour. It wasn't unknown for him to sit through a hearing with his features totally impassive and without saying a word. When he spoke in his summing up his mouth scarcely moved. However, even this imperceptible action provided such a contrast with his former state that at one trial a small girl in the public gallery called out excitedly, 'Daddy, Daddy, it's alive!'

Judges are not usually noted for their humour. Sir John Walter, Chief Justice of Wales during the turbulent years of the early seventeenth century, spoke for many of his profession when he answered Judge Denham's greeting, 'My lord, you are not merry,' with his famous reply, 'Merry enough for a judge.' Yet there have been exceptions and even the soberest incumbents of the bench have not resisted the occasional *bon mot* at some time in their career. Lord Ellenborough presided over a trial once at which a very nervous young barrister rose to make his first address to a court. 'My lord,' he began, 'my unfortunate client . . . my lord, my unfortunate client . . . my lord, my unfortunate . . . my lord . . .'

'Go on, sir, go on,' said the judge, 'as far as you have proceeded hitherto, the court is entirely with you.'

Sir Fletcher Norton, whose discourtesy was notorious throughout the profession, was engaged by a client contesting what he claimed were his manorial rights. The case was heard by Lord Mansfield who had suffered before from Norton's rudeness. At one point the case got bogged down and in an effort to get it moving again Sir Fletcher volunteered, 'My Lord, I can illustrate the point in an instance in my own person. I myself have two little manors.'

'We all have good reason to know that, Sir Fletcher,' remarked the Lord Chancellor.

During Judge Malins' time as Vice-Chancellor he had a fellow Vice-Chancellor named Bacon. At the end of one trial presided over by Malins the disappointed litigant against whom he had just passed judgement hurled an egg at his head. The missile missed by some considerable distance and Malins quietly observed that 'That must have been intended for my brother Bacon in the next court.'

Sir Nicholas Bacon, a judge of great standing in the sixteenth century made an equally felicitous use of his own name when hearing an appeal by a man named Hogg against his death sentence. The prisoner sought to win the judge's favour on the grounds that they were related.

'Nay, my friend, you and I cannot be kindred except you are hanged,' said the judge. 'For a hog is not bacon until it is well hung.'

A dispute in opera circles centred on a singer's ability to appear in a forthcoming production finally ended up in front of Lord Darling before whom a string of 'expert' witnesses were called to express their opinions on the artiste's skill. In cross-examination one of them admitted, 'He doesn't sing like the Archangel Gabriel.'

'I have never heard the Archangel Gabriel sing,' commented defence counsel, Henry Duke.

'That is a pleasure yet to come, Mr Duke,' the judge told him.

Judge Toler (later Lord Chief Justice of Orbury) had scant regard for members of the bar. When an impoverished Dublin barrister died many of the city's lawyers clubbed together to pay for his funeral. Toler was approached and asked to donate a shilling. 'Only a shilling?' he asked. 'Only a shilling to bury an attorney? Here's a guinea; go and bury another twenty of them.'

On his appointment to the bench Mr Justice McCardie was entertained by a large gathering of legal friends to celebrate his success. When it came to his turn to speak the new judge remarked, 'I am especially glad to see here tonight those hundred solicitors each of whom sent me my first brief.'

The old custom of the delivery of the assize sermon was one part of the legal tradition that most circuit judges would happily have dispensed with. Lord Chief Justice Baron Yelverton was one forced to endure a long, tedious assize sermon delivered in an icy, cold church one Sunday in March. As he was leaving the vicar asked eagerly what he had thought of the address from the pulpit.

'Wonderful, my dear friend,' replied Yelverton, 'it passed all human understanding, and I thought it would have endured for ever.'

In 1859 when rumours were circulating in Westminster that Lord Campbell had been created Lord Chancellor, his friend and colleague, Sir Richard Bethell (later Lord Westbury) caught sight of him in Westminster Hall wearing a large fur coat to combat the cold wind outside. Pretending not to see Campbell he walked past until stopped by his friend's, 'Mr Attorney, don't you know me?'

'I beg your pardon, my Lord,' said Bethel. 'I mistook you for the Great Seal.'

For many years Lord Alverstone, a former Lord Chief Justice, was a member of the choir of Kensington Parish Church. During his time as Attorney-General an American tourist attended morning service one Sunday with the sole purpose of seeing the distinguished lawyer. Having difficulty in identifying him among the rest of the choir she beckoned the verger and asked him to point out Lord Alverstone.

'Well, ma'am, you see there's me and the vicar,' he apologized, 'but as for the rest of the choir, well, so long as they behave themselves we make no enquiries as to their antecedents.'

Mr Justice Morris, the proud owner of one of the richest Dublin accents in the legal profession of his day, attended the wedding of a daughter of a fellow judge in London and fully entered into the spirit of the occasion. As the happy couple were leaving, the sentimental Irishman said to a friend, 'I wish I had a shoe to throw at them.'

'Never mind, old boy,' said his companion, 'why not throw your brogue?'

During Lord Herschell's time on the woolsack, Lord Fitzgerald, a Lord of Appeal, was approached by one of the Lord Chancellor's fellow Jews who complained that his legitimate claims for a judgeship had been overlooked.

'My deal fellow, what would you expect from a Jew but a passover?' replied Fitzgerald.

Not long after Charles Evans Hughes was made Chief Justice of the US Supreme Court his first ruling caused a sensation when upheld the rights of Californians to fly a red flag. While public interest was still buzzing with his decision Hughes was tackled by F. W. Wile, a leading newspaperman at the time, when they met by chance at a Washington garden party. Wile asked the newly elected judge how he'd taken to the widespread praise he'd received for having blossomed out as a liberal.

'Wile,' answered Hughes, 'I blossomed out a long time ago. But the trouble is, it never bore fruit.'

A judge in a Kentucky courtroom was having trouble controlling the public gallery and eventually bellowed from the bench, 'Silence in court! Half-a-dozen men have been convicted already without the court's having been able to hear a word of testimony.'

Mr Justice Plowden was asked by a barrister at a social gathering if he had ever tried gin and ginger-beer. 'No,' replied Plowden, 'but I've tried a lot of chaps who have.'

As Mr Justice Cardozo was stepping from the bench at the end of one court sitting, he slipped, bumped down several steps and landed heavily on the floor. 'I hope your Honour is not hurt,' said an anxious court official, helping the judge to his feet.

'No, my honour is safe enough, but the seat is bruised confoundedly,' said the judge as he rubbed the offended area.

The ardent golfing judge, Mr Justice Lawrance, asked a boy who stepped into a witness-box to give evidence whether he was 'acquainted with the nature of an oath'.

'I ought to; ain't I your caddie?' answered the boy brightly.

The American judge, Justice John M. Harlan, was asked by a young attorney how it was possible to assess evidence. Harlan gave this novel answer: 'Usually in conflicting evidence one statement is far more probable than the other, so that we can decide easily which to believe. It is like the boy and the house-hunter. A house-hunter getting off a train at a suburban station, said to a lad, "My boy, I'm looking for Mr Smithson's new block of semi-detached cottages. How far are they from here?"

'"About twenty minutes walk."

'"Twenty minutes! Nonsense, the advertisement says five."

'"Well, you can believe me or you can believe the advertisement, but I ain't trying to make a sale."'

Judge Avory, questioning a witness in his usual stern manner, asked, 'Let me see, you have been convicted before, haven't you?'

'Yes, sir, but it was due to the incapacity of my counsel rather than to any fault of my own.'

'It always is and you have my sincere sympathy.'

'And I deserve it seeing that you were my counsel on that occasion.'

A defendant at the Old Bailey who was accused of being in possession of burglar's implements such as a screwdriver, a jemmy and sticky tape, explained to Judge Lawrance, 'They are the tools of my trade, my Lord.'

'That is precisely what the prosecution alleges,' said his lordship.

An Irish witness who was paying scant regard to the oath he had taken and was consequently deviating widely from the path of truth was brought up short by the judge who told him, 'Look here, sir, tell me no more unnecessary lies. Such lies as your attorney advises you are necessary for the presentation of your fraudulent case I will listen to, though I shall decide against you whatever you swear, but if you tell me another unnecessary lie I'll put you in the dock.'

Lord Alverstone was afflicted by slight deafness in later life though he struggled valiantly to prevent this from affecting his work at the bench. In the course of one trial he experienced great difficulty in hearing one of the witnesses and at one point, cupping his hand behind his ear, asked, 'What was your last sentence?'

'Six months,' was the prompt reply.

An American judge renowned for his tenderness towards defendants was on the point of passing sentence on a craven man, whimpering pathetically in the dock. 'Have you ever been sentenced to imprisonment?' he enquired.

'No, your Honour,' replied the wretched man, with tears in his eyes.

'There, there,' comforted the judge. 'You're going to be now.'

At the end of his trial a Yorkshire man was awarded a conditional discharge and ninety hours' community service. In addition the Recorder at York Crown Court gave him this piece of advice: 'I think you should give up burglary. You have a withered hand, an artificial leg and only one eye. You have been caught in Otley,

Leeds, Harrogate, Norwich, Beverley, Hull and York. How can you hope to succeed?'

The District Attorney of Bronsville, Texas, suffered the ignominy of being sent to prison for driving while under the influence of alcohol. But what made the case even more intriguing was the DA had actually sent himself behind bars. The trouble arose after the car he was driving smashed into the crash barrier while he was driving along one of the roads in the area under his jurisdiction. At the police station he signed a complaint against himself, and, at what could legitimately be called an extraordinary hearing, he charged himself with drunken driving and then pleaded guilty. He was duly fined $50 and given ten days in the cells.

A young woman brought before an Iowa court for driving through a red light asked the judge to deal with her case as quickly as possible as she was a school teacher with classes waiting for her at that moment. 'You're a school teacher?' said the judge mischievously. 'Madam, I shall realize my lifelong ambition. I've waited years to have a school teacher in this court. Sit down at the table and write "I went through a red light" five hundred times.'

A butler found guilty of the heinous crime of stealing his master's wine was told by Lord Kenyon, passing sentence, 'Prisoner at the bar, you stand convicted on the most conclusive evidence of a crime of inexpressible atrocity – a crime that defiles the sacred springs of domestic confidence, and is calculated to strike alarm into the breast of every Englishman who invests largely in the choicer vintages of Southern Europe. Like the serpent of old, you have stung the hand of your protector. Fortunate in having a generous employer, you might without dishonesty have continued to supply your wretched wife and children with the comforts of sufficient prosperity, and even with some of the luxuries of affluence; but dead to every claim of natural affection and blind to your own real interest, you burst through all the restraints of religion and morality, and have for many years been feathering your nest with your master's bottles.'

Mr Justice Heath was one of the notorious band of hanging judges who hanged in all capital cases on the grounds that he could think of no secondary punishment. 'If you imprison at home,' he declared, 'the criminal is soon thrown upon you again hardened in crime. If you transport, you corrupt infant societies and sow the seeds of atrocious crimes over the habitable globe. There is no regenerating of felons in this life, and for their own sakes, as well as for the sake of society, I think it is better to hang.'

Mr Justice Maule was about to pass sentence on a defendant found guilty of a serious offence when the man broke in with the plea, 'May God strike me dead, my lord, if I did it.' The judge waited some considerable time, looking sternly at the defendant, until he finally broke his silence with the remark, 'As Providence has not seen fit to interpose in your case, it now becomes my duty to pronounce upon you the lighter sentence of the law.'

'It is difficult to see how I can be a forger when I can't even sign my own name,' pleaded a defendant before Sir John Ross.

'You are not charged with signing your own name,' was his Lordship's curt reply.

Sir Henry Dickens, the son of the novelist, led a distinguished legal career which culminated with his elevation to the bench. There he was addressed by a persistent habitué of the dock on whom he was about to pass sentence. 'You ain't a patch on your dad,' shouted the defendant.

'I quite agree with you, but what do you know about my father?'

'Oh, I've read all 'is books.'

'Really, where?'

'Well, I read some in prison.'

'Have you. That's capital, for you will now have eighteen months in which to resume your studies.'

Prolix Lord Esgrove condemning a traitor to death for the murder of a soldier elaborated on the defendant's crime with the remark, 'And not only did you murder him, whereby he was bereaved of his life, but you did thrust, or pierce, or project, or propel the lethal weapon through the belly-band of his regimental breeches, which were the property of his Majesty.'

A court in Wyoming was asked to try the case of local schoolmaster whose dedication to poetry almost equalled his devotion to the bottle. 'Ye're charged with bein' drunk and disorderly,' said the magistrate. 'Have you anything to say why sentence should not be pronounced?'

'Man's inhumanity to man makes countless thousands mourn,' said the teacher. 'I am not so debased as Poe, so profligate as Byron, as ungrateful as Keats, so intemperate as Burns, so timid as Tennyson, so vulgar as Shakespeare, so . . .'

'That'll do,' said the magistrate, 'seven days. And officer, take down the names of the others he mentioned and round 'em up. They sound as bad as he is.'

A defendant described by Mr Justice Lawrance as 'a professional burglar' and sentenced by him as such, took exception to the epithet and complained, 'I dunno what you mean! Professional! I've only done it once before, and I've been nabbed both times.'

'Oh, I don't mean to say that you had been very successful in your profession,' retorted the judge.

Judge Jeffreys, described by Charles II as having 'no learning, no sense, no manners, and more impudence than ten carted street-walkers' became notorious for his ruthless treatment of Monmouth's rebel forces at the Bloody Assizes that followed their débâcle at Sedgemoor in 1685. Pointing his stick at one of the accused as he entered the witness-box, he said, 'There is a rogue at the end of my cane.'

'At which end, my lord,' answered the defendant stoutly.

A 44-year-old Austrian kleptomaniac who had spent half his life in prison decided to end it all when it became clear that he could never be cured, and put both of his hands into a prison workshop machine, severing them at the wrists. The court which heard his subsequent trial sentenced him to another four years behind bars.

Lord Erskine during one cross-examination said to the witness, 'I will now lay aside the role of the advocate and address you as a man.'

'You will do nothing of the sort,' the judge told him sharply. 'The only right and licence you have to appear in this court is as an advocate.'

Summing up has been described as: 'The process in which the judge detracts from and discounts counsels' multiple arguments, makes his own deductions, adds his own wisdom, divides the blame, and roundly charges the jury to deliver a square result.' A vivid illustration of this principle was given by the judge at the end of the trial of a man accused of horse-stealing. The defence counsel, Mr Plowden, had been absent from court when the prisoner pleaded 'guilty'. After a word with the judge, however, the plea was changed to 'not guilty' and the trial proceeded. When the judge came to his own final address he said, 'Gentlemen of the jury, the prisoner at the bar is indicted for stealing a horse. To this charge he has pleaded guilty, but his learned counsel is convinced that this was a mistake. The question is one, therefore, for you gentlemen which you believe. If you should have any doubt, pray bear this in mind, that the prisoner was there, and the learned counsel wasn't.'

Lord Bramwell was not a judge who relished listening to the tedious pleading of counsel that dragged on past the court's normal adjournment time and when the barrister defending a farmer charged with shooting at a boy stealing apples eventually came to the end of his long-winded and gratuitous appeal to the jury his Lordship delivered his own curt summing up as follows, 'I shall leave the case to you in eight words. The prisoner aimed at nothing and missed it.'

Mr Justice Swift, who would never have classified himself as a teetotaller, presided over the trial of a man who had taken a small Scotch and soda on New Year's Eve, had another for the road just after midnight and had then been stopped on the way home and charged with drunken driving. In his summing up Swift laid the case before the jury. 'Now, what are the facts?' he asked. 'Why, this man had one drink in 1933, and didn't have another until 1934.'

The jury returned a verdict of 'Not guilty'!

At the end of his trial before Mr Justice Maule a defendant was asked whether he wanted to call any witness and replied, 'None but my Maker, who is well aware of my complete innocence.'

'Gentlemen,' said Maule to the jury, 'the prisoner is charged with stealing a watch. He calls a witness who does not appear. On the other hand, two witnesses saw him take the watch. Consider your verdict.'

Mr Justice Vaisey once remarked, 'It is a fearful thing to contemplate that, when you are driving along the road, a heavy horse may at any moment drop from the sky on top of you.'

Some judges have delivered some pretty odd rulings in their time on the bench. There was one who once observed that, 'What would be a nuisance in Belgrave Square would not necessarily be so in Bermondsey.' There was a coroner who told the court at the end of an inquest, 'It seems to me a shame that they cannot make regulations on the Continent identical with those in this country.' And another of his fellows recorded an open verdict on a recent death with the comment, 'In many years' experience I have made the observation that if a woman is going to commit suicide she rarely takes her handbag.'

In the Michaelmas term of 1607 Sir Thomas Holt took one Astrigg to court for the accusation that 'Sir Thomas Holt struck his cook on the head with a cleaver, and cleaved his head; the one part lay on one shoulder, and another part on the other.' The defendant pleaded 'not guilty' but the case went against him. In an appeal the decision was reversed when the defence argued successfully that the words used did not state categorically that the cook was dead. The appeal court agreed with this interpretation, stating that for the words to be counted as slanderous their accusation had to be direct. As it was, the court ruled, there was a suggestion that the cook was still living, in spite of the wound he had received, in which case the indictment was 'but trespass'. On this basis they found for the defendant.

When Mr Justice Oliver was called upon at Manchester Assizes to give a ruling on an unusual case involving an injury sustained by an innocent passer-by, he decided that a cricket ball struck for six which flew out of the ground and struck a woman on the head could not be regarded as a nuisance.

Awarding damages claimed under a 1934 Act a British judge told the jury that damages were awarded for the loss of a happy life. He went on to say that the court had to take into consideration the fact that the life of a criminal could not be construed as a happy one. He therefore announced that he would award damages of £187. Counsel for the 'criminal' seeking damages had originally applied for £500.

When three High Court judges were asked to rule on whether driving a car on to a policeman's foot rendered the driver guilty of assault they were unable to agree on an answer.

Opening a trial in a rough and ready mining town in Nevada during the last century, the judge, a man noted for his integrity throughout the West, told the court, 'Gentlemen, this court has received from the defendant a cheque for $10,000. He has received from the plaintiff in the case a cheque for $15,000. The court has returned $5,000 to the plaintiff and will now try the case on its merits.'

A distinguished judge asked to explain the difference between law and equity courts replied, 'At common law you are done for at once; at equity you are not so easily disposed of. One is prussic acid, and the other laudanum.'

In 1954 shop premises in Inverness were flooded as the result of an extraordinary chain of events. A cow waiting to be auctioned at a cattle sale held in the street outside, broke out of her compound through an unsecured gate, climbed a flight of stairs over the shop, fell through the floor above the shop and in struggling to free herself turned a tap which flooded the shop. The shop-keeper took the auctioneers to court to claim damages but the judge ruled against him since he found himself 'forced to the conclusion that a gate-crashing, stair-climbing, floor-bursting, tap-turning cow is something *sui generis* – the only one of her kind – for whose depredations the law affords no remedy unless there was foreknowledge of some such propensities.'

A judge presiding over a case in which a couple living together as common law man and wife were jointly charged with a variety of offences spoke to the defendants sternly before passing sentence.

'I am not very sympathetic to couple living together when they are not married,' he said. 'I think it is immoral and can lead to crime.'

At the end of a month-long trial in New York, Judge Daly acquitted three defendants charged with disturbing the peace. They had been arrested by one of the city's policemen who had noticed Jan Tice, a 27-year-old model standing in the nude on the corner of Liberty Street and Broadway, together with John Wilcock and Eugenie Lewis who were taking photographs of her. In their defence the trio said that they were preparing a book about New York's tourist attractions in which the comely Jan would feature prominently in front of all the buildings. To Detective Joseph Leary this was clearly a breach of the peace and the three went to trial. After hearing the evidence from both sides, however, the judge found for the defence, arguing that in the eyes of the law Detective Leary could not technically be classified as the public. He continued, 'Actually the defendants annoyed no one, interfered with no one, obstructed no one, except perhaps the police officer . . . A breach of the peace requires the presence of the public. The public relates to people. There weren't any people there.'

Counsel pleading before Lord Darling that his client had an unblemished reputation apart from one crime, 'a slight case of murder' was told by the judge, 'Unfortunately I have sentenced to death too many persons who bore the highest character to enable me to give that argument more than its due weight.'

A highwayman named Bolland who was imprisoned in Newgate before his trial sensed that the gallows might not be far away and sent for a lawyer to see if there was any way he could get off the charge. 'By getting a doctor to make an affidavit of your illness,' he was told. A suitable doctor was duly found and in exchange for fifty guineas Bolland received his affidavit which read, 'The deponent verily believes that if the said James Bolland is obliged to take his trial at the ensuing sessions, he will be in imminent danger of his life.' Unfortunately for Bolland it was not money well spent. The judge to whom the plea was presented replied that he certainly believed the doctor's opinion to be the case and the trial went ahead immediately.

In later life Mr Justice Park developed the habit of thinking aloud. In the course of one trial in which an elderly woman was accused of stealing faggots his lordship muttered, 'Why, one faggot is as like another faggot as one egg is like another egg.' The sharp-eared defence counsel heard these 'thoughts' and made good use of them in his summing up, carefully repeating the judge's words. 'Stop,' shouted the judge excitedly. 'Stop! This is intervention of Providence. That was the very thought that had pass through my mind. Gentlemen, you must acquit the prisoner.'

The following exchange was recorded in a law report from a few years ago:

Judge: I suppose the word 'horse' in the rule does not include an aeroplane?

Counsel: No, I think not.'

Judge: It ought to, it is much the same thing.

Counsel: I think that it was put in for the relief of the archdeacon.

Leading American attorney, Max Steuer, was forced to apologize to a court one day but managed to turn even this to his advantage.

He rose with dignity, bowed to the bench and said, 'Your Honour is right and I am wrong, as your Honour generally is.'

Lord Hewart delivered the following ruling after hearing a tedious argument from a verbose barrister, 'Counsel for the appellant has raised six points in support of this appeal. In the first point there is nothing, and the same applies to the others. Five times nothing are nothing. The appeal is dismissed.'

When Lord Young was told once that the House of Lords had, on appeal, affirmed a decision of his, he replied, 'It may be right for all that.'

The judge in a Chicago court ruled that certain evidence presented before him was inadmissible which greatly annoyed the attorney concerned, who insisted there was nothing wrong with it. 'I know your Honour, that it is proper evidence,' he complained, 'Here I have been practising at the bar for forty years, and now I want to know if I am a fool?'

'That,' replied the judge quietly, 'is a question of fact, and not one of law, and so I won't pass upon it, but will let the jury decide.'

A British judge asked to give a ruling on a case involving the burning of a human body, answered, in the words of *The Times*, 'that the consumption by fire of the mortal remains of homo sapiens was not the subjection of goods and materials to a process within section 271 (1) (c) of the Income Tax Act, 1952'.

In the days when Oliver Wendell Holmes sat on the bench of the US Supreme Court an attorney from Wyoming brought his case before the court and argued an impassioned appeal with all the majesty and vocabulary of the Wild West. In spite of his best endeavours he lost the case, but the clerk of the court noticed how much the judges had enjoyed his submission and having over-heard Holmes whisper to fellow judge Charles Evans Hughes, 'Can't we hear that old bird again?' advised the attorney to apply for a rehearing. This was granted and the Wyoming lawyer began his second attempt, 'I come to you as John the Baptist saying: "Repent ye, repent ye." '

'But are you not aware of what happened to John the Baptist?' asked Justice McReynolds who was enjoying the performance as much as Holmes.

'Yes, I am quite aware,' replied the frontier man. 'He lost his head through the influence of a harlot. But I know the Supreme Court would not be so influenced.'

On another occasion Justice Holmes wrote a majority decision of the Supreme Court in a famous case which upheld the statute in the State of Virginia that provided for the sterilization of imbeciles. Only one member of the Supreme Court refused to lend his name to this ruling, Roman Catholic judge, Justice Pierce Butler. Holmes is reported to have commented to a colleague on Butler's decision, 'He knows the law is the way I have written it. But he is afraid of the church. I'll lay you a bet the Church beats the law.'

A Harvard professor who often read Holmes's opinions to his law students used to offer them this one as follows: 'Three generations of imbeciles are enough. Mr Justice Butler dissenting.'

Mr Justice Matthew, trying the case of a man who put his trust in a rights of way issue on the notice 'Private Road' which he had erected, told the plaintiff, 'What's the good of that? Whenever I see "Private Road" stuck up, I know it's a short and easy cut, and go down it. Why did you not build a wall across it?'

Lord Ellenborough had to preside over a case in which a leading counsel was arguing a long and dreary property dispute. He was still addressing the court when the adjournment time came and consequently asked their lordships when it would be their pleasure to hear the remainder of the argument.

'We are bound to hear you out, sir,' Lord Ellenborough told him, 'and I hope to do so on Friday, but, alas, pleasure has long been out of the question.'

The case of *Hall* v. *Hyder* had important implications for licensees subject to English law. The case concerned the consumption in licensed premises of a glass of shandy by a person under eighteen. The justices who had first heard the case ruled that no offence had been committed since the shandy was not intoxicating liquor as defined by the 1964 Act, since the prosecution had not shown that it was of a strength exceeding two degrees proof. In an appeal the case went before the Lord Chief Justice who reversed the earlier decision. His Lordship argued that the licensee had sold beer and, quite independently, lemonade. This he was obliged to do by the law, for according to section 163(1) of the 1952 Act, he could not sell beer diluted with any other substance, as the Act stated, 'If any dealer in or retailer of beer dilutes any beer or anything to beer other than finings for the purpose of clarification he shall be liable to a penalty of fifty pounds . . .' According to the Lord Chief Justice this had also prevented the mixing of weaker beer with stronger beer unless the publican mixed 'half and half' in the customer's presence and at his request. Under these circumstances, he explained, the publican was acting as the consumer's agent. The same apparently applied to the serving of shandy. The publican sold beer and lemonade (or in some cases ginger-beer) and then, at the customer's request mixed the two. From this premise his Lordship argued that beer had therefore been sold, in spite of the fact that it had been consumed as a mixture with another liquid. In reply to the claim that the mixture had resulted in a new liquor, the Lord Chief Justice explained that this did not alter the fact that beer had been sold for consumption on the premises and under these circumstances the law had been broken.

Of the many criticisms levelled at the bench one of the most persistent is that judges in the past haven't always paid their full attention to the cases tried before them. In the most extreme instances the judges have actually fallen asleep in court, which has led to some harsh rebukes from both the bar and their fellows. Lord Bowen, told of a learned colleague, who made a regular habit of dropping off after lunch, snoozing until 3.30 at which time he came to and immediately adjourned the court. Coming to his defence Bowen replied, 'It is as it should be, he obeyed the hymn "Shake off dull sloth and early rise".'

Towards the end of a trial which had become notorious for its length the defence counsel made an impassioned appeal for the case to be abandoned on the grounds that the judge had been asleep for over two hours. 'Nor is this the only occasion on which I have been prompted to the foregoing allegation,' he continued. 'The court official in question has been slumped over his arms with both his eyes closed on no less than sixteen occasions in the last 63 days.

'I agree that the cross-examinations, particularly my own, have been exceptionally boring. Last Thursday, which you will remember was particularly hot, the judge appeared to fall asleep on four occasions — before and after lunch. Acting on his example, I noticed eight of the jurymen in a similar posture.

'I know that the judge and jury slept during the trial of Robert Emmet; that, however, was during the summing-up. But how can a judge who is asleep assess the credibility of a witness?

'The judge may reply that he was only simulating sleep the better to evaluate the evidence. But justice must be seen to be done.'

His colleague joined in with the claim that he had been obliged to asked for a 'toilet adjournment' at one stage in the proceedings in order for the judge to be roused from his apparent sleep.

When Lord Bowen was told on one occasion that the Lord Chief Justice with whom he had been sitting on the bench had recently been more wakeful than usual, he replied that he had heard comments to the effect that the Lord Chief Justice had been troubled with occasional attacks of insomnia.

After 49 years' service in the California Supreme Court, Judge Marshall McComb was sacked following growing complaints from a wide section of the State's legal profession. A colleague spoke for all when he said of the judge, 'Things have gone too far. Hardly has Marshall hit the bench when he goes to sleep. Last week I nudged him, he shook himself awake and slipped out of the court: we thought that he had gone to relieve nature but an usher told us he was placing a bet by telephone.' Further investigations into the judge's suitability to remain on the bench revealed that he had recently eaten a green paper napkin instead of his salad.

Magistrates frequently come off no better than judges in the eyes of the public, though according to one legal textbook, 'Merely to impute want of ability to a Justice of the Peace is not actionable without proof of special damage, for ability is not essential to that office.'

A letter returned to the magistrates' court on the Wirral had pencilled on the envelope, 'We know we're good – but we're not that good.' The message had come from a Post Office sorter who had found it was addressed to a man of 'no fixed abode'.

Local magistrates granted a drinks extension until midnight to an Oxfordshire hotel which was the venue for a dinner-dance organized by Alcoholics Anonymous.

A Richmond magistrate told his court one day that homosexuality was a serious subject. In his opinion no one was justified in writing a novel about it at the moment. It should be dealt with seriously, he emphasized.

After hearing a 50-year-old defendant claim that he had to beg for money in order to buy food, a magistrate in Cheltenham reached into her handbag, took out her purse and handed half-a-crown to a policeman, with the instructions that the man was to be put on a bus to Gloucester. 'We don't want beggars here,' she explained.

A former magistrate at Marylebone Police Court named Broderip, considered himself something of an authority on natural history. In one hearing of an affiliation order, he found against the defence and granted the application. However, before leaving the court he called over the losing counsel and said to him, 'You made a very good speech and I was inclined to decide in your favour, but you know I am a bit of a naturalist. While you were speaking I was comparing the child with your client, and there could be no mistake. The likeness was most striking.'

'Good heavens,' said the barrister, 'my client was not in court. The man you saw was my clerk.'

A Surrey magistrate set on giving a defendant before him a light sentence asked the man about to be bound over if he had any friends who could act as sureties. 'The Almighty is my friend,' the man replied.

'Yes, yes, but the point is can you give us the name of a friend living near?'

'The Almighty is everywhere.'

'I know, but I am afraid we shall have to think of someone of more settled habits.'

The landlady of the Victoria Hotel, Ramsay, Isle of Man, landed herself in trouble when she joined with her customers who were having a sing-song. The good lady had forgotten that her premises were not licensed for singing. The stipendiary magistrate told her that by breaking into song the landlady had 'abandoned the neutral attitude' which would have kept her within the law. She was accordingly fined ten shillings for providing an entertainment for which she had no licence.

Ten shillings was also awarded as a fine against a young London painter who drove a borrowed car across a canvas spread out in a Kensington mews. He claimed that he was creating an action painting but the court were only interested in his driving without a licence.

A well-known Marylebone magistrate named Plowden had an enviable reputation for disposing of cases with admirable speed. A colleague asked for the secret and was told, 'It's all very simple, and an ideal arrangement. My clerk listens without deciding, while I decide without listening.'

A man leaving a magistrates' court having just been fined £18 for driving a car without a valid road fund licence noticed that another car parked outside was displaying a tax disc that had also expired. This car, it turned out, belonged to the magistrate who had imposed the fine.

The father of a schoolboy who was constantly dodging lessons was told by Walsall magistrates that they shared his frustrations at being prevented by law from giving the boy a sound hiding. 'We feel sorry for you,' said the chairman. 'If you cannot do it yourself, get a friend to half beat the life out of the lad. It will do him the world of good, and if they summon you for hitting him come before this bench and we will know what to do.'

A policeman giving evidence to magistrates at Glossop handed them four sheets of paper numbered one to four. He then told the court that as he had been walking along his beat one of the youths in the dock approached him and swore. His words were written on the first sheet of paper. On speaking to the youth, he swore a second time. The police directed the bench to the second sheet. Asked if he knew what he had said was an offence the youth replied with the words written on sheet number three and when told that he would be reported he replied with the remark written on sheet number four.

Hooliganism at country dances in Cumberland had reached such a scale that Carlisle magistrates resolved to take a tough line in stamping it out. The court paid great interest therefore in a case involving the throwing of eggs at a local hop. The principal prosecution witness claimed that two rotten eggs were thrown; however, the defence counsel vigorously asserted that the eggs were fresh.

For all their faults the incumbents of the bench can seldom be blamed for not allowing justice to be seen to be done and here are two graphic examples of that noble principle.

A circuit judge trying a burglar who had been caught in possession of a pair of handcuffs decided that the cause of justice would be greatly advanced if he demonstrated to the jury 'how handcuffs could be used to incapacitate a victim'.

Paying no attention to the repeated objections of the prosecuting counsel the judge closed one handcuff round one wrist and shut the other round his second wrist. Only at this stage was the prosecutor able to break in with the disquieting news that the keys were still missing. The case had to be adjourned while his lordship was taken to a locksmith.

A former Master of the Rolls, Sir William Grant, was one of the most patient, if taciturn, judges ever to sit on a British bench. In one memorable case he listened for two days to an elaborate argument laid before the court on the interpretation of a particular Act of Parliament without saying word. Only when counsel had finished his submission to the complete satisfaction of both himself and the court did the judge open his mouth, and then it was only to say, 'Gentlemen, the Act on which the pleading has been found is repealed.'

During his time as a circuit judge Lord Mansfield had to preside over a case of witchcraft brought against a poor old woman whose neighbours had joined forces in an effort to get rid of her. So strong was the feeling against her in the court that Mansfield decided to hear the evidence against her without comment and to do as little as he could to irritate those present. Accordingly he listened to neighbours claiming under oath that they had seen her walking in the air, upside down. At the end of the trial he reviewed the evidence calmly. 'I do not doubt that this woman has walked in the air with her feet upward, since you have all seen it,' he told them, 'but she has the honour to be born in England as well as you and I, and consequently cannot be judged by the laws of the country, nor punished but in proportion as she has violated them. Now, I know not one law that forbids walking in the air with her feet upward. We all have a right to it with impunity; I see no reason, therefore, for this prosecution, and this poor woman may return when she pleases.'

A 25-year-old workman who had the misfortune to get on the wrong side of a bulldozer took his case to court in an effort to gain damages. Mr Kenneth Jones, QC, representing the claimant, told the court that the accident had affected his amorous adventures.

The judge asked if the man was married and when counsel answered 'No' his lordship replied, 'Well, I can't see how if affects his sex life.'

The quality of mercy

I don't care to speak ill of any man behind his back, but I believe the person who has just taken his departure to be an attorney.

Dr Samuel Johnson

Attitudes towards practitioners of the law vary according to which side of a judgement fate casts you. While it may be true, as was once suggested in *Puck* magazine, that 'ignorance of the law does not prevent the losing lawyer from collecting his bill', most lawyers try to follow Quintillian's advice, 'the advocate who seeks to persuade should first seek to please'. And it's in pleading his case that the advocate, be he barrister or solicitor, has to use all his guile and oratory.

There are times when counsel have to open their case by apologizing for their client's absence, which can get them off on a bad footing at the outset. Some manage to get over this problem. A solicitor who rose to address a police court in Middlesbrough to apologize for his client who had been unable to attend the hearing said, 'In the first place he is a man of not very bright intellect. Secondly he is employed on important government work.' While on a similar note a barrister faced with explaining the non-appearance of a key witness told the court, 'There are several reasons, m'lud, why the witness in question is unable to attend, the first being that he is unfortunately dead.'

Defence counsel faced with the seemingly impossible task of pleading on behalf of a bank robber who had been caught red-handed nevertheless sought to impress the mitigating circumstances on the jury. 'The man is basically innocent,' he began confidently. 'Upon entering the bank he subsequently robbed, he got his foot jammed in the revolving door and had to be helped to the counter by the lady he then threatened. On being told that the till did not contain the £5,000 for which he had asked, he reduced his demands, first to £500, then to £50, and finally to £5 and the offer of a drink around the corner.'

Another inspired plea came from counsel for a firm of food processors who submitted that the casual presence of a caterpillar in a tin of peas was 'an unavoidable consequence of the process of collection or preparation of food'. This proved no more successful than the former.

At the inquest held into the death of a Bermondsey man who had been knocked down and killed by an army motor-cyclist, counsel appearing for the War Office told the coroner, 'The Secretary for War wishes to express his deep regret at this tragedy. The Secretary is deeply disturbed that his department should be concerned in any way with the shortening of human life.'

An interesting case of hit-and-run came before a Surrey Court some years ago. The plaintiff gave evidence that he had been crossing a street in Guildford when he heard a shout, turned round and saw a cow thundering round the corner. The animal knocked him to the ground, trampled over him and made off. Counsel defending the cow's owners submitted that the person in charge of a tame animal was not liable for damage done by it which was 'foreign to its species'. He told the court that he would prove that the cow attacked the passer-by, which, if it was the case, would relieve the owners of any liability. At this point the judge asked, 'Is one to abandon every vestige of common sense in approaching this matter?'

'Yes, my lord,' replied counsel.

The hearing was adjourned.

A Scots girl employed at a fish factory at Eyemouth was charged with ill-treating the prawns she converted into scampi. On her first court appearance the girl admitted the offence (which amounted to putting prawns on a hot plate) but having taken legal advice she changed her plea to 'not guilty'. The solicitor representing her challenged the action brought against her on two counts.

He referred to section 13 of the 1912 Protection of Animals (Scotland) Act, under which 'animals' were classified as any domestic or captive animal. There was no mention of prawns.

Then, under another section of the same Act, he indicated that it referred to birds, fish and reptiles in captivity. If a prawn was to be classified as a fish, he argued, according to the Act it had to be one in 'captivity', in other words, one living in an aquarium. He told the court that he had examined a standard natural history book and had been unable to find any evidence that a prawn could be classified as a fish.

On the basis of this submission the presiding sheriff indicated that if it was established that a prawn is not a fish the prosecution would have some difficulty in proving its case.

Rufus Choate, an eloquent American advocate, once represented a blacksmith who, having failed in business, was loaned some iron by a friend in order to start up again, only to have the iron seized by a creditor. The consequence of this action was that the friend sued for the recovery of his iron and the blacksmith found himself in court. When it came to his turn to speak, Choate employed his oratory to great advantage. 'He arrested the arm of industry, as it fell towards the anvil,' he said directing his gaze at the unfortunate blacksmith. 'He put out the breath of his bellows. Like pirates in a gale at sea, his enemies swept everything by the board, leaving him, gentlemen of the jury, not so much as a horseshoe to nail upon his door post to keep the witches off.'

All were moved, though none more so than the blacksmith. Tears came into his eyes and when a friend asked what was the matter, he replied, 'I had no idea I had been so much abused.'

A Mr David Mackenzie Ross, defending counsel in a very sensitive case told the court that people tend to think of rape in 'a rather Victorian way'. He added, by way of explanation, 'We tend to get over-censorious about it. Rape is an emotive word in so far as women tend to put great stress upon it as being something unpleasant.'

A barrister defending a man charged with being drunk in charge of a bicycle attempted to prove that a bicycle could not be classified as a 'carriage', thus absolving his client of the crime of being 'drunk while in charge on any highway . . . of any carriage'. Inventive as his plea was, it failed to win favour with the court, possibly because his case was based on the rhyme:

It won't be a stylish marriage,
I can't afford a carriage,
But you'll look sweet upon the seat
Of a bicycle made for two.

Picking winkles from a puddle on a mudflat landed one unfortunate beachcomber in court. His counsel pleaded that no crime had been committed since winkles couldn't be considered fish, but the judge disagreed with him, arguing that an earlier ruling had established oysters as fish and that winkles and oysters were in the same category.

This forced counsel on to another tack, arguing that the puddle in the mudflat couldn't be construed as 'private water'. Here again the judge had an answer. Since puddles normally contain water and since this puddle was on private land, in the eyes of the law the winkles had been taken from private water. In the face of this ruling the defence was helpless and the winkle picker was found guilty and fined.

During his time as a practising lawyer Abraham Lincoln was approached by a man who wanted him to act on his behalf in a claim to retrieve several hundred dollars. Lincoln examined the case and found that, though likely to succeed, it would result in the ruin of a widow and her six children. He then wrote to the would-be client, 'We shall not take your case, though we can doubtless gain it for you. Some things that are right legally are not right morally. But we will give you some advice for which we charge nothing. We advise a sprightly, energetic man like you to try your hand at making six hundred dollars in some other way.'

An eager American attorney presented with a complicated brief spared no effort in his pre-trial research. He consulted authorities as far back as Julius Caesar and came to the court with an intricate and minutely detailed case. He spoke for well over an hour during which time he noticed the court's attention gradually wandering. As he approached the crucial part of his case he saw that the judge was looking completely nonplussed so he broke off and enquired, 'Your Honour, I bet your pardon; but do you follow me?'

'I have so far,' the judge replied wearily, 'but I'll say frankly that if I thought I could find my way back, I'd quit right here.'

Lord Russell of Killowen was following a similarly intricate line of argument in one of his pleas when the judge broke his flow by asking, 'What's your authority for that statement?'

'Bring his lordship a book on elementary law,' said the barrister testily to the usher.

Following his arrest for his revolutionary views John Thelwell the eighteenth-century English reformer, found himself charged with treason. Writing to Lord Erskine, then the country's most celebrated barrister, he said laconically, 'I shall plead my own case.'

'You'll be hanged if you do,' Erskine replied.

'Then if I do, I'll be hanged,' was Thelwell's answer.

When the verdict in a closely contested case found in favour of the defendant his solicitor thought it his duty to cable the unexpected news to his client who was unable to attend through illness. 'Justice has triumphed' was his simple message.

'Appeal at once,' telegraphed the client in reply.

Before his spell as American ambassador to Britain at the turn of the century, Joseph Choate established a formidable reputation in New York courts. In one case his opposing counsel was an attorney from Westchester County, representing a man from White Plains. His case was weak and to buttress it he resorted to trying to turn the jury against Choate, warning them not to be taken in by his 'Chesterfieldian urbanity'.

When it came to his turn to speak Choate returned the compliment by warning the jury not to be influenced by his opponent's 'Westchesterfieldian suburbanity'.

At the end of a trial held on the South Wales Circuit the defence counsel asked Lord Bramwell, who was presiding, whether he could address the jury in Welsh. The evidence showed that a verdict of 'guilty' was as good as given and his lordship agreed to the request, albeit with some reluctance. The barrister spoke briefly and the jury were out for a matter of minutes before they returned a remarkable verdict of 'not guilty'. Lord Bramwell was dumbfounded and after the court had been cleared he asked the recorder for a translation of the counsel's remarks. It read, 'This case, gentlemen, lies in a nutshell. You see exactly how it stands. The judge is an Englishman, the prosecuting counsel is an Englishman. But you are Welsh, and I am Welsh, and the prisoner is Welsh. Need I say more?'

In addition to his skill at the bar Abraham Lincoln was renowned for his story-telling, as one court clerk recalled after the former attorney had been elected President.

'I was never fined but once for contempt of court. Davis fined me five dollars. Mr Lincoln had just come in, and leaning over my desk had told me a story so irresistibly funny that I broke out in a loud laugh. The judge called me to order, saying, "This must be stopped. Mr Lincoln, you are constantly disturbing this court with your stories." Then to me, "You may fine yourself five dollars." I apologized but told the judge the story was worth the money. In a few minutes the judge called me to him. "What was that story Lincoln told you?" he asked. I told him, and he laughed aloud in spite of himself. "Remit your fine," he ordered.'

Lord Darling, one of the most famous judges of the first half of this century, took a perverse delight in displaying his ignorance of contemporary life. Hearing one barrister refer in court to the Coliseum, his lordship enquired innocently, 'Isn't that the place where the Christians feed the lions?'

'I think your lordship must be thinking of the Trocadero,' replied counsel, 'where Lyons feed the Christians.'

The great Irish lawyer, John Philpot Curran found himself one day arguing in the Irish court of Chancery before Lord Clare, the Lord Chancellor. To Curran's intense annoyance the Lord Chancellor was clearly more interested in fondling the dog which always accompanied him into court than in paying attention to Curran's plea. When it was clear that his lordship had switched off completely Curran gave him a taste of his own medicine and stopped talking in mid-sentence.

'Go on, Mr Curran, go on,' said the judge.

'A thousand pardons, my lord,' replied Curran. 'I really took it for granted that your lordship was engaged in consultation.'

At the end of one of his cases Sir Edward Carson was taken aside by the judge who remarked on the extraordinary discrepancy between two witnesses Carson had called. One of them, a carpenter, had been lucid, articulate and informative. Whereas the second, a publican, had been everything a bad witness can be: equivocal, imprecise, forgetful and contradictory. When the judge had finished making these observations Carson smiled at him ruefully and mercly said, 'That is so, my lord. Yet another case of the difference between bench and bar.'

An Irish judge in one of the Four Courts approached Easter with such a backlog of work that he decided to take the unprecedented step of sitting on Good Friday. The members of the Irish Bar who had ideas of disappearing to their Easter haunts on that day didn't take kindly to the idea and protested vehemently.

'Better the day, better the deed,' argued the judge.

'Well, my lord,' said one of the rebellious counsel, 'you'll be the first judge who ever sat on Good Friday since Pontius Pilate.'

Judge Willes, one of the kindest and gentlest members of the bench, was frequently the target of bullying barristers. In one instance he was being browbeaten by a very persistent member of the bar who was gradually breaking down the judge's resistance to his application. In a desperate attempt to assert his authority Willes told the man, with little conviction, 'I am one of the most obstinate men in the world.'

'God forbid that I should be so rude as to contradict your lordship,' retorted the barrister.

Abraham Lincoln's engaging innocence shielded one of the shrewdest and most astute minds of the nineteenth-century American bar. As a colleague named Whitney later recorded, Lincoln had a rare skill in obtaining invaluable legal ammunition. 'I remember once,' Whitney wrote, 'that while several of us lawyers were together, including Judge Davis, Lincoln suddenly asked a novel question regarding court practice, addressed to no one in particular, to which the judge, who was in the habit certainly of appropriating his full share of any conversation, replied, stating what he understood the practice should be. Lincoln thereat laughed and said: 'I asked that question, hoping that you would answer. I have that very question to present to the court in the morning, and I am glad to find out that the court is on my side.'

One warm summer afternoon John Philpot Curran was addressing the county assizes in Limerick when the sound of a braying donkey came through the open windows and interrupted his speech. 'Excuse me, Mr Curran, one at a time, please,' said the judge drily. A short while later when his lordship was speaking to the jury at the end of the trial the donkey joined in again allowing Curran to say, 'I am sorry, my Lord, but there seems to be such an echo that I can scarcely make out what your Lordship is saying.'

Lord Mansfield, appointed Chief Justice of the King's Bench in 1756, was a man noted for his impartiality, which his sterner critics put down to his ignorance of the higher principles of the law. When confronted with the leading advocates of the day his lordship sometimes allowed his heart to rule his tongue. To Sergeant Davy who was arguing a knotty point before him once he was rash enough to comment without any justification, 'If this be law, sir, I must burn all my books, I see,' which allowed the sergeant to retort, 'Your lordship had better read them first.'

The clashes between F. E. Smith (later Lord Birkenhead) and the judges of his days at the bar are probably the best known examples of legal wit this century. Poor Judge Willes suffered at the hands of the young barrister on two notable occasions. During the course of one heated exchange he said crossly, 'You are extremely offensive, young man.' To which F. E. replied unabashed, 'As a matter of fact, we both are, and the only difference between us is that I am trying to be and you can't help it.'

Another time the same judge asked testily, 'What do you suppose I am on the bench for, Mr Smith?'

'It is not for me to attempt to fathom the inscrutable workings of Providence,' replied the future Lord Chancellor.

Mr Justice Ridley remarked to F. E. Smith at the outset of a trial, 'Well, Mr Smith, I have read the pleadings and I don't think much of your case.'

'Indeed,' Smith answered, 'I'm sorry to hear that m'lud, but your lordship will find that the more you hear it, the more it will grow on you.'

When arguing before the Court of Appeal, F. E. was at pains on one occasion to explain his case in the simplest terms, a process which necessarily took far longer than the standard pleas. The Master of the Rolls objected to the barrister's patronizing manner and eventually cut him short with the rebuke, 'Really, Mr Smith, do give this court credit for some little intelligence.'

'That is the mistake I made in the court below, my lord,' he replied before resuming his plea.

Winston Churchill summed up F. E. Smith with the observation that he burned all his candles at both ends and as an undergraduate he gained one of the most distinguished firsts of his year. He worked as hard for his BCL and was justifiably put out when he was only awarded a second. Many years later he found himself refusing silk to the Oxford professor who had awarded him a lower class after the oral part of his examination. Never one to miss an opportunity to settle a score, Lord Birkenhead, as he then was, told the unsuccessful applicant, 'Silk is only awarded to academic lawyers of distinction.'

Mr Justice Darling served as a barrister on the Oxford circuit and in his day was as impertinent as F. E. Smith. He found himself addressing the court in one trial long after the hour at which it normally adjourned. At five o'clock the chairman drew his attention to the time, 'Do you notice the hands of the clock, Mr Darling?'

'They seem to me, sir, to be in their normal position at this time of day,' was the bland reply.

When on the bench Darling displayed a distressing ignorance of everyday life. From one barrister, of whom he asked, 'And who is George Robey?' he received the polished reply, 'He is the Darling of the music-halls, my Lord.'

Edwin James was one of the bar's most gifted advocates before disgrace forced his removal. In happier times he was attempting to cross-examine a witness against a volley of interruptions from the bench which were seriously jeopardizing his attack. When the judge eventually finished James remained seated and the witness left the box. The judge asked if he had any more questions to put, to which the furious barrister replied coolly, 'Oh, yes, my Lord, I have, but I am waiting for your lordship to call your next witness.'

As a young lawyer Thaddeus Stevens lost a case in an out-of-the-way court in Pennsylvania through a very questionable ruling. He was so livid when the verdict was announced that he threw his books and papers to the floor, grabbed his hat and made for the door in high dudgeon. The judge halted him and asked with an air of insulted majesty if he intended to express his contempt for the court. Stevens bowed politely and answered, 'No sir; I am trying to conceal it, your Honour, but I'm finding it damned hard to do.'

During the trial of *Woodcock* v. *Bird*, presided over by Lord Chief Justice Jervis at Warwick, the judge remarked to the prosecuting counsel, Mr Hayes, that 'it was a pity that two birds couldn't live in harmony'.

'Yes, it is, my lord,' replied Hayes, 'but my client complains of the length of the plaintiff's bill.'

Not that lawyers themselves are free from accusations of over-charging their clients. John Gay wrote a short poem on the subject, entitled *The Lawyer*:

> A fox may steel your hens, Sir,
> A trull your health and pence, Sir,
> Your daughter may rob your chest, Sir,
> Your wife may steal your rest, Sir,
> A thief your goods and plate.
>
> But this is all but picking,
> With rest, pence, chest, and chicken;
> It ever was decreed, Sir,
> If Lawyer's hand is fee'd, Sir,
> He steals your whole estate.

There is even an amusing story of a man who was refused legal aid in order to sue his barrister for professional negligence. As a result of further enquiries, however, he was granted a legal aid certificate to appeal against the decision to refuse him legal aid in the first place!

A popular story of the American bar concerned one of its most successful members at the turn of the century, who had his portrait painted depicting him standing in a familiar posture with one hand in his pocket. A former client, seeing the picture, commented that it would have been far more life-like if the artist had portrayed the lawyer with his hand in another man's pocket.

An indication of the outrageous charges made by some lawyers comes from one notorious demand sent by an anonymous solicitor to one of his clients:

> To crossing the Strand after seeing you on the other side to discuss your case with you – 6s 8d
> To re-crossing the Strand after discovering the person was not you – 6s 8d

From the American Mid-West comes the story of a small town lawyer at work at his desk one day when the local butcher burst through the door and demanded, 'If a dog steals a piece of meat from my shop, is the owner liable?'

'Certainly,' answered the lawyer.

'Very well, your dog took a piece of steak worth half a dollar about five minutes ago.'

'Is that so,' said the lawyer. 'Then if you care to leave the other half with my clerk, that will cover my fee.'

Clarence Darrow, a great American criminal lawyer, who became known as 'The Great Defender', established a reputation for pulling off remarkable acquittals. After one such triumph the woman whom he had been defending approached him and asked, 'How can I ever show my appreciation?'

'My dear woman,' said Darrow, 'ever since the Phoenicians invented money there has been only one answer to that question.'

The American railroad baron, E. H. Harriman, was a man of immense wealth, power and influence. He was also regarded as one of the foremost 'malefactors of great wealth' the West had ever known. At the climax of one enormous deal a problem arose over the legality of the merger proposed. Harriman immediately cabled the respected corporation lawyer, John G. Johnson, and sparing no expense sent a detailed outline of the project that filled sheets of telegram forms. Harriman was worried that he might be prosecuted under Federal legislation that restricted schemes of the sort that had made his fortune. He told Johnson that money was of no concern in sending his reply, the important point was to have an answer immediately, so that the deal could go through. Within a day of receiving the frantic enquiry Johnson sent his reply. It read, 'Merger possible; conviction certain.' According to popular account those four words of advice cost Harriman $100,000 – $25,000 a word.

A young American lawyer struggling to get started in his profession was no doubt grateful to his legal training when one creditor wrote to him:

> 'Dear Sir, Kindly advise me by return mail when I may expect a remittance from you in settlement of my account.'

Without further ado the lawyer replied:

> 'Dear Sir, I have your request for your advice of recent date, and beg leave to say that not having received any retainer from you I cannot act in the premises. Upon receipt of your check for $250 I shall be very glad to look the latter up for you and acquaint you with the results of my investigations. I am, sir, with respect, your most obedient servant.'

A young English barrister who had the satisfaction of winning his first case concerning a pair of stolen trousers, went to his client in the dock and said with justifiable pride, 'Congratulations. You are a free man. You can leave now.' The look of relief on the defendant's face slowly gave way to one of anxiety as he eyed the prosecution counsel.

'I'd rather wait until the prosecutor leaves the court,' he muttered nervously.

'Why?'

'Because I've got them on,' he whispered.

A New York judge called a very nervous young attorney to him at the start of a trial having watched the young man lay his hat and coat on the bench. 'Is this the first time you've practised in this court?' asked the older man.

'Yes, your Honour,' replied the attorney suddenly aware that he might have committed some breach of etiquette.

'Then get your hat and coat and put them where you can keep an eye on them,' the judge told him.

The weight of age and experience was brought to bear with devastating results at the end of another New York trial when an over-enthusiastic young lawyer spent five hours summing up his client's case. When he finally sat down the jury were against him to a man and the seasoned old counsel opposing him sensing this, merely said in his final plea, 'Your Honour, I will follow the example of my young friend who has just finished, and submit the case without argument.'

Reputations at the bar are made and broken by counsel's power and skill in cross-examination. Sir Edward Carson could be crushing when the circumstances suited him. When practising in

Ireland he demolished one prime prosecution witness with just four questions:

'Are you a teetotaller?' he asked.

'No, I'm not.'

'Are you a moderate drinker?'

The witness gave no answer.

'Should I be right if I called you a heavy drinker?'

'That's my business.'

'Have you any other business?' said Carson finishing his questioning and resuming his seat with an air of supreme confidence.

F. E. Smith once acted on behalf of a tram company which was taken to court by the parents of a small boy who had been knocked down by one of its vehicles. According to the prosecution the boy had been so severely injured that he was unable to raise one arm higher than his head, and when he stood in the witness-box to tell his sad tale to the court the little fellow presented a pitiful sight. When his turn came to cross-examine the boy, F. E. Smith was conscious of the great sympathy that he had aroused in the court, so it was in the gentlest and most encouraging tone that he put his questions, 'Now, my boy, your arm was hurt in this accident?'

'Yes, sir.'

'And you cannot lift your arm high now?'

'No, sir.'

'Would you mind showing the jury once more how high you can raise your arm since the accident?' whereupon the boy lifted his arm with obvious discomfort until it was shoulder high. 'And how high could you raise it before the accident?' asked F. E. innocently. Up shot the arm straight over the boy's head.

A farmer in America who had lost a colt to one of the earliest railway companies in the Mid-West took the case to court to reclaim damages. When he was asked by the counsel for the railroad company how much the horse had been worth, he answered unwaveringly, 'Not a cent less than $500.'

'It was pedigreed stock, I suppose?' asked the attorney.

'Well, not exactly,' admitted the farmer grudgingly, 'but you could never judge a colt like that by its parents.'

'Quite so,' replied the lawyer. 'I've often noticed how crossing one with a locomotive will improve the breed.'

A man who had received a blow on the head which he claimed had subsequently caused great physical and mental distress went into the witness-box to give evidence and found himself cross-examined by Frank Lockwood, who asked, 'Were you really sick or did you only feel sick?'

'Well, it's the same thing, isn't it?'

'Oh no,' said Lockwood. 'M'learned friend is sick with me, very sick, but I don't expect that he will throw up his brief.'

A famous barrister named Campbell Foster was summing up his case to a jury when he noticed that his opposing counsel, Digby Seymour, was showing no interest in what he was saying and was actually carrying on a none too discreet conversation. 'Pray, Mr Saymour, be quiet,' said Foster angrily.

'My name is not Saymour, it's Seymour,' replied the offending barrister.

'Then, sir, see more and say less,' countered Campbell Foster.

When Oxford City Council sold a plot of land to a housing development company they didn't reckon on the new owners building walls to mark the boundaries of their land and when the walls went up the Council took the law into their own hands and demolished them. Not unnaturally the housing company resented this cavalier approach and took the Council to court where they were represented by Sir Wilfred Greene. In his summing up he painted the corporation in a very bad light arguing that when they sold the land, 'they omitted, whether by accident or by design, to reserve to themselves rights of way over certain roads, the sites of which were indicated on the relevant plans. Their omission to do so has led them to perform a variety of manoeuvres in seeking some possible expedient which would enable them to obtain, against the will of the company, the rights for which they had failed to stipulate. The last expedient which commended itself to the corporation consisted of a judicious combination of the provisions of the Private Street Works Act of 1892 and the City's steam-roller. To what extent this miserable performance can be reconciled with the dignity of a great and historic corporation is a question which may well be left to the more sober reflection of the City Fathers. We are not concerned with it.'

On a lighter note are the summings up of four Irish barristers which may have done little to advance their clients' causes but which must have brought a little light relief at the end of their respective trials:

'Gentlemen of the jury, it will be for you to say whether this defendant shall be allowed to come into court with unblushing footsteps with the cloak of hypocrisy in his mouth, and draw three bullocks out of my client's pocket with impunity.'

'There is no use in the learned counsel trying to throw dust in your eyes by dragging a red herring across the trail.'

'And when we come to Brown. Ah, there the impudent and deceitful fellow stands, just like a crocodile, with tears in his eyes, and his hands in his breeches pockets.'

'Gentlemen, the charges against my clients are only mares' nests, which have been traced to their birth, and are found to have neither origin nor existence.'

An American lawyer acting on behalf of a man charged with housebreaking presented his case to the court with the novel argument that he did not break into the house at all because all he had done was insert his arm through an open window and remove a few small articles. 'Now my client's arm is not himself,' argued the lawyer, 'and I fail to see how you can punish the whole individual for an offence committed by only one of his limbs.'

It took the judge several minutes to ponder this plea before passing sentence. 'This case has been well argued. Following it logically, I sentence the defendant's arm to one year imprisonment. He can accompany it or not as he chooses.'

The defendant chose not to follow his wayward limb and with his lawyer's assistance detached the artificial arm and leaving it in the dock walked from the court.

Next witness please

Gentlemen of the jury if you believe the witnesses for the plaintiff you will find for the plaintiff. If you believe the witnesses for the defendant you will find for the defendant. If, like myself, you don't believe any of them, Heaven knows which way you will find. Consider your verdict.

Mr Justice Maule

Judges have always had an ambivalent attitude towards witnesses. Back in the eighteenth century Judge Perrot addressed the jury at the end of a trial concerning the rights to a certain stream with these remarkable words:

> Gentlemen, there are fifteen witnesses who swear that the watercourse used to flow in a ditch on the north side of the hedge. On the other hand, gentlemen, there are nine witnesses who swear that the watercourse used to flow on the south side of the hedge. Now, gentlemen, if you subtract nine from fifteen, there remain six witnesses wholly uncontradicted; and I recommend you to give your verdict accordingly for the party who called those six witnesses.

Others have been less willing to accept either a witness's evidence or his credentials. One distinguished judge presiding over a case involving robbery was obliged to listen to a doctor called as an expert witness for the defence. The doctor told the court that in his opinion the defendant was suffering from kleptomania and added pompously, 'And, your lordship, of course, knows what that is.'

'Yes,' replied the judge sternly, 'it is what I am sent here to cure.'

Exchanges from the witness-box, whether with the bench or the bar have enlightened many otherwise humdrum hearings and, though laymen in the midst of experts, many witnesses have scored impressively off both opponents.

Judge Hawkins, who was known to be more patient with witnesses than most counsel, found himself during one cross-examination fast losing his temper with a barrister's vain attempts to keep a garrulous old lady on some pattern of ordered thought. In the end he interposed and asked what he considered to be a perfectly straightforward question.

'It's no use bothering me,' snapped the witness, 'I've told you all I know.'

'That may be,' said the judge, 'but the question rather is, do you know all that you have told us?'

An American witness was asked to tell the court what he found at the scene of a crime. 'Naught but barren nothingness, as Shakespeare says,' he replied.

'Never mind what Shakespeare says!' thundered the judge. 'If he knows anything about this case he can be summoned!'

Witness: Can you tell me what kind of bird this is?
Mr Justice Matthew: Well, my friend, if there is any truth in the adage that birds of a feather flock together, I should say it was a gaolbird.

During his time as Chief Justice Lord Ellenborough once had occasion to reprimand a witness for appearing in court in his working clothes.

'I beg your Lordship's pardon,' replied the witness unflinchingly, 'but I am every bit as properly dressed as you. You come here in your working clothes and I in mine.'

A western farmer who was giving evidence to an American court at the turn of the century seemed to the judge to be weighing his testimony unquestioningly towards the accused. The judge stopped him at one stage and asked, 'Do you know the nature of your oath?'

'Sure,' answered the farmer.

'Do you know you are not to bear false witness against your neighbour?'

'I'm not bearing false witness against him,' retorted the farmer. 'I'm bearing false witness for him.'

Judges will sometimes take the side of a witness, and when the resourceful advocate, Serjeant Ballantine, was heckling a witness more than the judge thought fitting, he checked this, saying, 'Really, this is a long way from the point.'

'I am well aware of that, my lord,' replied Ballantine. 'But if I were to begin any nearer, the witness would discover my object.'

After being called to the witness-box in a Kansas courtroom a witness took his oath and was then told by the defence counsel, 'Now, sir, stand up and tell your story like a preacher.'

'No, sir!' interrupted the judge. 'None of that; I want you to tell the truth.'

Following the unfortunate disappearance of some sizeable deposits, a London bank was taken to court and in the course of the trial several of those who had suffered from its carelessness gave evidence. As one of the men was entering the witness-box to take his oath he stumbled.

'I hope you are not hurt,' said the judge.

'Oh no, my lord, I have only lost my balance,' was the man's reply.

A famous Victorian circuit judge who had the habit of lightening his hours on the bench by dreaming up puns had a field day when confronted by a witness named Gunn. The man seemed reluctant to speak out at first which allowed his Lordship to goad him on with an encouraging, 'Come, come, Mr Gunn, don't hang fire.' And when he came to be dismissed the judge's passing shot was, 'Mr Gunn, you can go off. You are discharged.'

A case of pig-stealing that came before a court in Ireland presided over by Mr Justice Lawson featured a strong defence that laid great emphasis on the accused's good character. A succession of neighbours, priests, friends and well-wishers went into the box to swear to his good name and upstanding reputation. When it came to his summing up, Mr Lawson took note of their testimonies and told the jury, 'Gentlemen of the jury, I think the only conclusion you can arrive at is this: the pig was stolen by the prisoner who is the most amiable man in the country.'

Mr Justice Swift found himself watching an amusing exchange during a case where a nervous junior was cross-examining a lady who repeatedly called him 'my lord'. This rattled the young man to such an extent that he finally snapped, 'Really, my good woman, you must not call me "m'lud"'.

'Ah,' commented Swift benignly, 'you must not be angry with the witness; let us hope it is only a little intelligent anticipation.'

Before accepting testimonies from children judges frequently make sure that they understand the full implications of the oath they are about to take. Sir John Ross accordingly asked one little girl who stepped into the witness-box if she knew what an oath was and what would happen to her if what she swore was untrue.

'Yes, my lord,' she answered confidently, 'I would not be given any witness expenses.'

'How old are you?' the judge asked a lady witness.

'Thirty.'

'Thirty! I have heard you give the same age in this court for the last three years.'

'I'm not one of those people who say one thing one day and another one the next.'

The great American lawyer, Samuel Leibowitz, took a special delight in discrediting witnesses called by the opposite side, who had clearly been primed for their task. Confronted by one oafish thug on whose evidence an important case depended, Leibowitz listened intently to all the man had to say throughout a very long testimony. His concentration was well rewarded for among the otherwise boorish recitation Leibowitz caught odd phrases that were quite out of keeping with the man's normal speech. 'I heard a weird, uncanny sound, a gasp, a cackle', and 'he was all of a flutter' were just two. When his own turn came Leibowitz had little difficulty in convincing the court that only a coach could have put phrases like those into the witness's mouth and as a result he proved that the witness had committed perjury by repeating a prepared story.

Samuel Leibowitz once sought to test a witness's veracity by confronting him with the tools of his professed trade. The man, an important witness at the scene of the crime, explained his presence by virtue of the Eskimo pies he claimed to have been selling. Only a short time after he had given his evidence and while he was still on the stand, Leibowitz sent outside for twenty Eskimo pies and nonchalantly distributed these to the judge, the jury and others in the court. The ice-creams were eaten in full view of the defendant who failed to recognize either them or their wrappers. Furthermore he was unable to explain how the ice-creams had been prevented from melting when he was allegedly selling them, which convinced the court of his perjury and won Leibowitz the case.

Sir John (later Lord) Coleridge was engaged in cross-examining a Miss Kennedy, a Mother Superior of a convent from whose order a nun had recently been expelled for certain violations of the code. In the course of his questioning Sir John remarked, 'You say that amongst her offences was the eating of a few grapes.'

'Yes,' replied Miss Kennedy, 'grapes are forbidden in a community consisting of nuns who have taken the vow of poverty.'

'But surely eating a few grapes is not a crime?'

'That depends upon the point of view. After all, Sir John, we all know what happened because a certain person ate an apple.'

Under cross-examination by defence counsel a farmer whose pigeons had been shot by the accused adopted a distinctly cautious tone.

'Now are you prepared to swear that this man shot your pigeons?' challenged the lawyer.

'I didn't say he shot them,' said the farmer. 'I said I suspected him of doing it.'

'Ah, now we're coming to it. What made you suspect the man?'

'Well, first, I caught him on my land with a gun. Secondly, I heard a gun go off and saw some pigeons fall. Thirdly, I found four of my pigeons in his pocket, and I don't think the birds flew there and committed suicide.'

Counsel are always trying to make witnesses appear with a straight 'yes' or 'no', but as most witnesses have found there are some questions that don't lend themselves to such glib replies. One brow-beating barrister, told as much by a stubborn witness, immediately demanded, 'I defy you to give an example to the court.'

'Are you still beating your wife?' replied the witness without hesitation.

A clever barrister was cross-examining an apparently dim-witted policeman about the arrest of his client. 'What exactly was the prisoner doing?' he asked.

'He was arguing with a taxi-driver.'

'Ah, do you think that proves he was drunk?'

'No,' agreed the constable. 'But you see, there wasn't a taxi-driver there.'

The following exchange took place at a trial in Chicago in 1938:
Counsel: Now, sir, did you, or did you not, on the date in

question or at any time, say to the defendant or anyone else that
the statement imputed to you and denied by the plaintiff was a
matter of no moment or otherwise? Answer me, yes or no.'
Witness: Yes or no, what?

A young constable, giving evidence in court for the first time, had
carefully read his notes to the court concerning a case of burglary
and was ready to face cross-examination. The first question, 'Who
was in the house?' threw him completely and the only reply he
could produce did little to impress those present. 'Please, your
worship, I was the only person present in the house except
another constable who was outside.'

Cross-examination often causes violent disagreement between
opposing counsel. In one case tried before Judge William
Douglas the prosecuting counsel asked a witness, 'And you say
you called on Mrs Jones, May second. Now will you tell the jury
just what she said?'

'I object to the question,' shouted the defence lawyer jumping
to his feet.

There then followed an hour's argument between them and
the judge, with Douglas finally allowing the question.

'And as I was saying,' began the prosecuting counsel, 'on May
second you called on Mrs Jones. Now what did she say?'

'Nothing,' replied the witness. 'She was not at home.'

The eminent American lawyer, Max Steuer opened his cross-
examination of a witness with the question, 'You are a barber, are
you not?'

'I am a tonsorial artist,' came the reply.

'Well, now, isn't that splitting hairs?' said Steuer.

'My lord,' said a witness to Mr Justice Maule, 'you may believe me or not, but I have stated not a word that is false, for I have been wedded to truth from my infancy.'

'Yes, sir,' said the judge gravely, 'but the question is, how long have you been a widower?'

Tim Healy scored a notable success when he discredited a witness put up by his opposing counsel as an expert on timber. Healy asked just two questions.

'What age are you?'

'Twenty-one.'

'How long have you been in the timber trade?'

'Two years.'

'A regular babe in the wood, my Lord,' said Healy, resuming his seat.

A carpenter subpoenaed to appear as a witness in an assault trial found himself cross-examined by an irascible barrister who tried every trick to discredit his evidence. At one point he asked the carpenter how far he had been standing from the parties in the fight when the first blow was struck.

'Just four feet five inches and a half away,' he replied.

'Pray tell me,' said the barrister, a note of cynicism in his voice, 'how is it possible for you to be so very accurate as to the distance?'

'Why to tell you truth, I thought that some fool or other might ask me, so I measured it,' he was told.

Sergeant Vaughan was notorious for the brow-beating he gave witnesses pitted against him. 'Where did you get that villainous face of yours from?' he asked one as soon as he'd taken the oath.

'From my father, sir.'

'And what was your father, pray?'
'A barrister, sir.'

'Are you acquainted with any of the people on the jury?' an American attorney asked a witness at the start of his cross-examination.

'Yes, sir, more than half of them.'

'Are you willing to swear that you know more than half of them?'

'If it comes to that, I'm willing to swear that I know more than all of them put together.'

Only a matter of months after representing a defendant Sir Patrick Hastings found himself cross-examining the same man in the witness-box during another trial. Sir Patrick, who had no recollection of their former acquaintance, chided the man after one reply, 'You will not give answers like that, if you take my advice.'

'I will not take your advice,' replied the witness sullenly. 'I took it once and it put me away for six months.'

Judge: The two men were fighting with chairs. Didn't you try to establish peace?
Witness: No, there was not a third chair.

An offensive barrister met his nemesis when cross-examining a police officer. 'When were you made Inspector?' he asked sarcastically.

'On the same day, sir, that you were made a QC,' replied the officer.

A sailor called to the witness-box to give evidence was asked by opposing counsel, Mr Hayes, 'Well, sir, do you know the plaintiff and the defendant?'

'I don't know the drift of them words,' the sailor replied.

'What! Not know the meaning of "plaintiff" and "defendant"? A pretty fellow you to come here as a witness! Can you tell me where on board the ship it was the man struck the other?'

'Abaft the binnacle,' said the sailor.

'Abaft the binnacle! What do you mean by that?'

'A pretty fellow you,' said the sailor, 'to come here as a lawyer, and don't know what "abaft the binnacle" means.'

'You say you saw the man stabbed in the hay-field with a fork. What kind of fork?' asked a junior, keen to break down the witness before him.

'Well, did you ever see a tuning fork or an oyster fork in a hay-field?' asked the witness in reply.

'You seem to have plenty of intelligence for a man in your position,' sneered Sir Fletcher Norton, cross-examining a witness.

'If I wasn't on oath I'd return the compliment,' the man replied.

Sir Edward Marshall Hall once asked a witness, 'Do you ever tell the truth?'

'I try to,' was the reply.

'Do you ever succeed?' enquired the barrister.

A New Zealand magistrates' court was told by a witness how he had helped a man wearing a bloodstained shirt push a woman's body into the back of a van parked in a picnic area at night. The witness explained that the body had been covered with a bedspread which was 'absolutely covered in blood'. He went on to say that he suspected foul play after the man had driven off without thanking him or even offering him a cigarette, which prompted him to call the police.

During a hearing into the collapse of a company in the early 1950s, an Assistant Official Receiver gave evidence on the firm's viability before it went into liquidation. 'I heard from two secretaries of the company that the sheriff's officer was so constantly in attendance that when he died the staff clubbed together and bought him a wreath. There seemed to be some doubt as to whether he was a member of staff himself.'

A Dundee schoolmaster was asked to give evidence in a case involving one of his pupils. During his cross-examination the teacher gave an inventory of the contents of the boy's pockets when he had been asked to empty them. These contained: two live wasps in an aspirin bottle; a gas-pipe 2½ feet long; 30 ball bearings, four spark plugs, two ounces of home-made gunpowder, three heavy bolts, five yards of bandage and the spike top of an iron railing weighing four lbs. He said that he had asked the boy why he had the gas-pipe and was told, 'I thought it might make an opium pipe like I have seen in pictures.'

Irish witnesses have been credited with many of the most amusing statements from the witness-box of which the following are a few examples:

'The prisoner said that were it not for soiling his hands, he would kick me into the street.'

Counsel: Were you in the vicinity of the accused when he committed the crime?
Witness: No, but I was standing next to him.

'There were two of us alone at the time.'

'He was sober enough to know he was drunk.'

Witness: The man was speechless drunk.
Counsel: How do you know he was speechless?
Witness: I could tell by his voice.

'After a fruitless search, your worship, we found all the money with the exception of the silver teapot.'

Towards the end of a murder case in which the defendant was represented by Samuel Leibowitz, the prosecution all but succeeded in proving that his alibi was false. Leibowitz's client claimed that he had been working in a fishmarket at the time of the murder, but when a selection of fish was brought into the court he couldn't identify a single one. When Leibowitz got up to address the jury for the last time the situation looked bleak.

'I want you, Mr Rabinowitz, and you, Mr Epstein, and you, Mr Goldfogel, and you, Mr Ginsberg,' he began, 'to explain to your fellow jurymen that fraud which has been perpetrated on my client. You see through it; they do not. Was there in all that array of fish a single pike, or pickerel, or any other fish that can be made into gefilte fish? There was not. My client told you that he worked in a store in 114th Street and Lexington Avenue. The prosecutor knows that is a Jewish neighbourhood, and he did not show a single fish that makes gefilte fish. What a travesty on justice! My client is an Italian who works in a Jewish fishmarket, and they try him on Christian fish.'

The jury were unanimous in their acquittal.

Have you anything to say?

One man is quite silent, another talks all the time, and twelve men condemn the man who has not said a word.
Chinese visitor on an English trial

British justice may appear to work in a perverse way but at least the onus is on the prosecution to prove a prisoner guilty, rather than the system which operates in some other countries where it is up to the defendant to get himself off the hook.

Nor is it true that the accused has no opportunity to speak for himself. There have been those eloquent defendants who have conducted their entire defence on their own, sometimes with great success. And even the lowly prisoner at the bar has occasionally managed to win a case by delivering a hard-hitting reply to the judge's question, 'Have you anything to say in your defence?'

Others have only been able to trot out mitigating excuses, but even if these have had no material effect on their own fate, they've certainly brightened many a dull hearing. And just once in a while a well-orchestrated protest from the dock can settle a case even before it's started.

At the start of an important social security fraud trial in Australia involving a cool 42 million dollars, the defendants were told that the prosecution had asked for it to be postponed for a year. This wasn't surprising since the defendants were 153 Australian Greeks and the police had so far been unable to distinguish which one was which.

After this nervous opening the proceedings erupted into pandemonium when one of the defence lawyers rose to his feet and admitted that he was unable to pronounce his client's name. It then transpired that the man had in fact committed suicide six months before. To add to the confusion two more lawyers then protested that they had both been briefed to defend the same man – at which they started grappling with each other and fighting over who was to have control of the papers on the case. This unseemly fracas was eventually brought to a halt when one of the defendants sprang from the dock and floored one combatant before holding aloft the other's hand, proclaiming that this was to be his counsel.

The proceedings broke up in total chaos, the defendants were all released and returned to their homes. The fraud went on as before.

Parking next to a fire hydrant is an offence in Los Angeles and Judge Richard Amerian didn't think a lot of the plea of innocence made by a 19-year-old driver brought before him after being booked for doing just this. He asked the accused to elaborate. 'The fire hydrant parked next to me,' was his simple reply. Anxious to let justice in his court be seen to be done, the judge ordered enquiries to be made with the City Works Department. These resulted in the driver's acquittal when it was proved that the equipment had been installed *after* the car had been parked.

When an American sentry on guard outside a Long Island army camp was attacked by a dog he tried to fend the animal off with his rifle. However, it kept going for him and in the end lunged at his leg and bit him on the calf. In self-defence the soldier killed the dog with his bayonet. It turned out that the dog was not only very valuable but that it belonged to one of the huge estates in the neighbourhood. The owner took the sentry to court to claim damages once it had been established that the bite was only superficial. After hearing depositions from both sides the judge asked the sentry, 'Why did you not knock the dog with the butt end of your rifle?'

'Why didn't the dog bite me with its tail?' answered the sentry, who was subsequently acquitted.

Horatio Bottomley was no stranger to bankruptcy petitions and writs, and was well accustomed to defending himself in court. He was once cross-examined by the Official Receiver: 'You keep racehorses?'

'No,' replied Bottomley.

'But you did keep racehorses?'

'No, never.'

'You have a place in Sussex called The Dicker?'

'Yes.'

'You have stables there – large stables?'

'Yes.'

'You bred horses there – racehorses?'

'Yes.'

'Then why did you tell me that you never kept racehorses?'

'I gave the correct answer. I never kept racehorses. They kept me.'

When F. E. Smith was created Lord Chancellor, Bottomley was one of the first to congratulate him, saying, 'Upon my soul, F. E., I shouldn't have been surprised to hear that you had been made Archbishop of Canterbury.'

'If I had, I should have asked you to come to my installation,' replied the new Chancellor.

'That's damned nice of you.'

'Not at all. I should have needed a crook,' replied F. E.

The Earl of Bradford was brought before an earlier Lord Chancellor to be examined in accordance with an application for a statute of lunacy brought against him. During their meeting the Lord Chancellor suddenly asked, 'How many legs has a sheep?'

'Does your lordship mean a live sheep or a dead sheep?' asked the would-be candidate for a straight-jacket and padded cell.

'Is it not the same thing?'

'No, my lord, there is much difference: a live sheep may have four legs, a dead sheep has only two: the two fore legs are shoulders; there are only two legs of mutton.'

('Though this be madness, yet there is method in't.')

After securing the acquittal of a pickpocket Montague Williams was approached by his client as he left the court. 'God bless yer, guv'nor,' said the man. 'I ain't paid you half enough for what you've done for me, but if you come along to Piccadilly and choose a little bit of jewellery, watch and chain or ring, I'll get it for you without any difficulty.'

Bromley magistrates' court cleared an RAF officer of a charge of driving while under the influence of alcohol after hearing how he had allegedly driven off a road into a wood. The defendant's obvious authority clearly carried weight both with the magistrates and the police. To the sergeant called to the scene of the accident the officer said smartly, 'Get this bloody tree out of the way; then I can press on.'

A well-known supplier of fresh local 'produce' suffered the inconvenience of being fined £300 for poaching by Shropshire magistrates. A short time afterwards notices began to appear in and around Market Drayton advising customers that owing to unforeseen circumstances he had been forced to increase the price of his pheasant, partridge, rabbit and venison.

When a West German woman found her husband slumped over the kitchen table after a drinking session she decided that he'd had his last chance, and shot him twice. That at least was the prosecution case when the woman, 37-year-old Frau Ingrid Nicken, appeared in court. However, the defence disputed the prosecution's charges, since fate had intervened in the Nicken's unhappy marriage and had carried off Herr Nicken with a heart attack before his wife fired a shot. How could she be guilty of trying to kill a man who was already dead, they argued? She was given two years for attempted murder, but appealed immediately against the verdict.

A county court in Dorset ordered a resident to fill in a hole which he had dug across a country lane near his home, and assumed that would be the end of the matter. So it came as a surprise when a second hole appeared in the same place only a few days later. This, it appeared, had been dug by the defendant's 78-year-old father, who proudly announced, 'The judge didn't say I couldn't dig one of my own.'

The victims of an attempted street robbery found themselves in court after they had successfully foiled their assailant. Giving his version of the incident the man explained to the court, 'He demanded that I give him my wife's purse. Telling him that the purse was in her basket, I bent down, put my hands up her skirt, detached her artificial leg and hit him over the head with it. It was not my intention to do any more than frighten him off but, unhappily for us all, he died.'

A charming story was reported from the Canterbury Crown Court where a lady appeared in the dock several years ago charged with failing to settle a £7 10s dress bill. The case was adjourned to allow enquiries to be made into her financial status which had been called into question after she had been delivered to the court in a Rolls Royce, albeit one that belonged to a friend. The glamour surrounding the case not to mention the defendant's own admirable attractions assured full press coverage complete with photographs. This had an unexpected result on its outcome. Before the next hearing an anonymous Frenchman paid the lady's fine adding in a note, 'Women of such beauty in my country are never guilty. I am sending the money, but if it has been paid, please get her some perfume.'

As it turned out the fine had not been paid and in accepting the Frenchman's largesse the judge reminded the defendant that two guineas costs remained outstanding and was to be settled within thirty days.

A Tennessee court was treated to a practical demonstration of assault and battery presented in the form of evidence during the trial of a powerfully-built young man accused on those accounts. The prosecuting counsel went out of his way to antagonize the defendant, but no matter how he goaded him the accused stolidly maintained that he had only pushed the plaintiff 'a little bit'.

'Well, about how hard is that?' asked the attorney.

'Oh, just a little bit,' replied the defendant.

'Well, for the benefit of the court, would you kindly step down here, and, with me for the subject, illustrate just how hard you mean.'

The prosecutor clearly hoped that his previous questioning would have annoyed the defendant so much that he would lose his temper in getting his own back and thereby seal his own fate.

The court watched as the defendant stepped down, walked up to the prosecutor and, as instructed, slapped him across the face, kicked his shin hard and, lifting him off his feet, threw him spreadeagled across the table. Then turning to the judge he said calmly, 'Your honour and gentlemen, about one-tenth that hard!'

Mr Justice Hawkins was presiding over a murder trial when the prosecuting counsel noticed the prisoner in the dock whispering to the policeman beside him. Counsel demanded to know what the defendant had said, but the officer demurred.

'Constable, inform the court what passed between you and the prisoner,' his lordship demanded.

'I would rather not, your lordship,' said the poor man with obvious embarrassment.

'Never mind what you would rather not do. Inform the court at once what the prisoner said,' demanded the judge.

'He asked me, your lordship, who that hoary heathen with the sheepskin was, as he had often seen him on the racecourse.'

The guilt of past crimes can hang heavily on a man's soul as was made apparent by an admission made by a defendant at a Southend Court that he had had one previous conviction. When asked what this had been for, he told the court that he had been found guilty of failing to produce his identity card while dressed in a bathing costume during the war.

The attentions of an ardent suitor had so distressed a divorcee that she applied for and was granted an injunction to prevent him from pestering her further. However, the man refused to give an undertaking that he would not try to see her, telling the court, 'I am prepared to marry her if she is willing.'

'In that case you will be remanded for a medical report,' the judge told him.

It has long been one of the anomalies of legal systems based on the British legacy of justice that prisoners in the dock are indicted solely on the count charged and with none other. I say anomaly, because at times this has led to some astonishingly brazen performances in the dock, of which this case, taken from an American trial is a good example. Samuel Leibowitz appeared on behalf of a defendant who he wished to prove had been framed for a crime which he didn't commit. Leibowitz set out to prove his client's innocence by impressing the man's apparent integrity on the court. He did that by demanding frank answers from him about his character.

'What is your occupation?' he began.

'Professional pickpocket.'

'How long have you been a professional pickpocket?'

'Twenty-four years.'

'If acquitted in this case, what will your occupation be in the future?'

'Professional pickpocket.'

But Leibowitz knew his jury well and his client was acquitted on the charge brought against him.

Two neighbours who took their domestic difference before Durham Assizes were clearly wasting the court's time after the judge had heard both sides of the case. He hinted as much to one of their counsel, asking whether his client would be prepared to settle the action quickly and if so what her price would be. Knowing that the lady was hard of hearing the barrister whispered to her in a voice that could be heard all round the court, 'His lordship want to know what you will take?'

'That's very kind of his lordship,' replied the woman. 'If it's no inconvenience, I'll take a light ale.'

A woman found guilty of unlawfully killing her husband with a kitchen knife applied for a widow's allowance. However, the High

Court, where her application ended up, ruled that she was not entitled to receive this in the same way as other widows whose husbands had passed away less intentionally.

Summoned to appear before the Woking bench on an affiliation order, a local man replied by letter, 'I don't know whether or not I'm the father of the child. I'm only an apprentice.'

The problems of trying to run a cinema in the Yorkshire seaside town of Whitby were vividly illustrated by a defendant who appeared in the dock of the magistrates' court to answer charges relating to two breaches of the safety regulations on his premises. 'I'm manager, book-keeper, operator two-thirds of the week, boiler attendant and maintenance engineer,' he pleaded, adding for good measure, 'I often have to catch mice by hand because of the lazy cat.'

Stroud magistrates heard almost as convincing a plea from a local driver charged with driving without due care and attention. 'My mind was preoccupied by the thought of my grandson who is in hospital with a broken thigh,' he told them. 'My brother who is seriously ill in another hospital, my wife who is caring for my 88-year-old mother-in-law and my sister, who has collapsed under the strain of looking after her – to say nothing of the stress involved in the reorganizing of local government.'

Having given a false name to the police a student brought before magistrates at Hartlepool was asked to account for his apparent dishonesty. 'I didn't think they would believe my name was Smith because I had no identification on me, so I told them my name was Jones,' he explained.

'My lord, how can I be called a quarrelsome man,' enquired a defendant charged with assault and battery, 'when I've been bound over twenty-three times to keep the peace.'

Asked to account for the dangerous condition of the wheels on his car a motorist in the dock at Malling magistrates' court, Kent, answered, 'When I tightened the wheel nuts before, I tightened them too tight, so when I went to tighten them again I thought if I didn't tighten them so tight they wouldn't be too tight, but I must have tightened them too loose.'

St Albans Divisional Sessions heard a police inspector ask a defendant summoned before them following a motoring con-tretemps, 'After the accident, why did you raise your bowler hat to acknowledge the driver of the car involved when you didn't know him?'

'The accident had caused the hat to become crammed down over my eyes and ears,' he replied, 'and – although it might have been polite to raise it to the other driver – I lifted it to alleviate my discomfort.'

Magistrates in Leamington Spa heard the tragic story of a 30-year-old housewife who was brought before them charged with stealing two tins of meat from a local supermarket. She had 'never been the same', she told them, following the shock of seeing a man running about in the nude. 'I have been under sedatives from my doctor ever since,' she added.

When a 76-year-old Yorkshire man was hauled before the Leeds magistrates on his 500th charge of drunkenness, he was given an absolute discharge. Two days later he appeared in court again on the same charge for the 501st time. In his defence he pleaded that he had been celebrating his anniversary. On this occasion the bench took a less lenient view and fined him 50p.

Prompted by an irresistible force an escapee from a Missouri mental hospital broke into a fried chicken stand in the town of Little Rock, Arkansas and ultimately ended up in the police station. There he told doctors, 'I heard voices telling me that if I did certain things I could marry Diana Ross.'

Before passing sentence on a convicted counterfeiter a judge asked if he had anything he wanted to say in his defence.

'The fact is, your lordship, the supply of the genuine article is so limited, and things generally so tight, a poor fellow must do something these times to turn an honest penny.'

A man arrested while attempting to break into a supermarket in Portsmouth also had to try and explain why he was standing in an alley stark naked. 'He had been trying to get into the supermarket next door but couldn't squeeze through the skylight,' alleged prosecuting counsel. 'He thought he would be able to get in if he took his clothes off – and that's what he did. He pushed his clothes through the skylight, intending to follow after them, but, to his dismay, he still couldn't get in.' In desperation he had shouted to a passing policeman, 'Get me out of here, I'm frozen.'

The defendant pleaded guilty to entering the supermarket with intent to steal and was fined £10 with £3 costs. On leaving the court he admitted, 'I had to shout to the policeman for help. What else could I do? It was daft but I'd been drinking a bit.'

Riding a bicycle to the common danger was the charge brought against a London cyclist nabbed by the police while riding along with both hands off the handlebars, reading a paper. 'It's the only chance I get of reading,' he said in his defence.

Forty years ago a defendant at Tower Bridge Court was fined five shillings for being drunk. During the hearing it was reported that he made his way into a telephone box, dialled 999, explained that he was very drunk and asked if a police car could come round and collect him.

The activities of an arsonist at Harrow School resulted in over £700 worth of damage and his subsequent appearance in court. There the 27-year-old defendant tried to argue his way into a light sentence by blaming his fundamental disagreement with the theory of relativity as expounded by Einstein.

While passing judgement on a notorious pickpocket a judge couldn't resist asking sarcastically, 'Just what good have you done society?'

'I've kept three or four detectives working full-time,' he replied.

An Irish magistrate determined to stamp out an epidemic of horse stealing in his area, and decided to frighten the life out of one convicted thief in the hope that this would impress the gravity of the crime on his like-minded fellows. 'Yours is a very serious offence,' he said gravely. 'Seventy years ago, it was a hanging matter.'

'Exactly,' replied the defendant. 'And seventy years from now who's to say it mayn't be a crime at all. Why not postpone sentence for a while and see how things work out?'

Tower Bridge Juvenile Court heard a case almost fifty years ago in which three young offenders pleaded guilty to stealing 7/1d from a car. The policemen who had apprehended them went on to say that they had thrown away 1/1d to make the division more manageable.

Drink of an unusual variety was the undoing of a man sentenced to four months' imprisonment by an Aberdeen court. The liquor in question was that used in ships' compasses for which the accused admitted he had a thirst amounting almost to an addiction. His sentence came as the result of making off with a gallon of the tipple filched from a trawler moored in Aberdeen harbour.

Only his quick thinking saved an Australian after he had been bitten by a snake on an outing to the bush. With no knife with which to open the wound and drain the poison he held his gun to his arm and shot himself to make the area bleed. He then managed to tie a string tourniquet round his arm before he passed out. Luckily he was found by walkers a short time later and was hurried to hospital where he made a good recovery.

Among his first visitors was a police detective who came to charge him with carrying a firearm on a Sunday. He was later fined £2 for this offence.

When a Birmingham businessman was asked to account for his unorthodox taste in leisure wear he told local magistrates, 'It relaxes me to wear a black bra under a see-through blouse, pantyhose, silver-plated heels and false eyelashes. Such things are worn every day by the London hippy jet-set men. I feel I am being discriminated against on grounds of age.' Enquiries into the last claim revealed that he was well over eighty.

Found guilty by a court in Fleetwood of stealing fish, a local man was fined £10, in spite of his plea that he had had to steal the fish to pay a £10 fine imposed on him earlier for receiving stolen fish.

You might not think there is anything unusual about a driver being fined for drunken driving and there wouldn't have been in the case of a farmer in Broken Hill, Australia, if he hadn't been apprehended driving a light aircraft down a public highway. His trouble started when he was spotted by a patrolling policeman flying so low over the town of Ivanhoe that the officer could see what the pilot was wearing. The policeman gave chase and headed out of town towards the airfield. On the way there he saw the aircraft coming back into town, this time down the road. He tried to get his car out of the way but in spite of pulling well to the side the aircraft's wing still scraped it as it sped by. When the pursuing officer finally caught up with the plane it was parked outside his own police station where the pilot was holding on to the wing to steady himself.

When the case came before the magistrates the farmer said in his defence that he had hit a bull as he was driving along the road and had gone to the police to report this!

'It is time you were checked in your career of crime,' a circuit judge told a burglar he was about to sentence. 'How many times have you been convicted for this offence before?'

'Five, my lord.'

'Five. Then this time I shall give you the maximum sentence laid down by the law.'

'Maximum? Don't regular customers get a bit of discount?'

A Scotsman brought before a court charged with causing a disturbance in an Aberdeen pub was asked why he had felt it necessary to bury a hatchet in the bar. 'I was having difficulty in catching the barmaid's attention,' he explained.

After listening to the evidence of a woman called to the witness-box by the prosecution a young defendant in a Boston court was told by the prosecuting counsel, 'You have heard what the last witness said and yet your evidence is to the contrary. Am I to infer that you wish to throw doubt on her veracity?'

'Not at all,' replied the man in the dock. 'I merely wish to make it clear what a liar I am if she is speaking the truth.'

Faced with a hardened thief who looked as innocent as a choirboy a county court judge had difficulty in reconciling his appearance to his occupation. 'Not only did you take all the money from the drawer, but it seems that you also helped yourself to a quantity of valuable jewellery. Is this true?'

'It is, my lord, but you will appreciate that I have always lived by the understanding that money alone does not bring happiness.'

Police in Italy broke up a cigarette smuggling ring and among those detained charged a Capuchin friar with handling contraband. When he appeared in the dock at Velletri Father Antonio Corsi expressed complete surprise, maintaining that he thought he'd been dealing with macaroni all along. Had he had any idea of the true nature of the merchandise he would have 'thrown it into the lake with my own hands', he assured the court.

After being caught using the same coin in his gasmeter for the best part of a year, a consumer told Bangor magistrates that he'd only acted 'on the spur of the moment'.

The only plea made by a defendant to a court in Yorkshire was one of total contentment as he outlined the circumstances that led up to the offence which landed him in court. The news that he was to become a permanent civil servant had just arrived. 'I could think of nothing else,' he said, 'I had just got everything I want in life.'

'Sheriff, I shot that pheasant because it was looking ill,' a Scotsman told a Musselborough court in answer to a charge of poaching.

During a trial in front of the West London bench one of the magistrates, Gervais Rentoul, asked the prosecutor, 'Is it true that you declared that the prisoner had stolen your pocket-book?'

'Your honour, I did not go as far as that. I merely said that if the prisoner had not assisted me in looking for the wallet, I might have found it.'

And, to return to the point where we started, with some defendants' ability to wriggle out of the clutches of the law, here is an example of philanthropy taken to extremes.

Baron Martin, probably one of the most good-natured judges ever to sit in a British court, was once obliged to pass sentence on a man convicted of petty theft. 'Look, I hardly know what to do with you,' he said, 'but you can take six months.'

'I can't take that, my lord; it's too much. I can't take it; your lordship sees I did not steal very much after all.'

'Well, that's very true; you didn't steal much. Now then you can take four. Will that do – four months?'

'No, my lord, I can't take that either.'

'Three?'

'That's nearer the mark, but I'd rather your lordship would make it two, if you'll be so kind.'

'Very well, then, take two; and don't come again. If you do I'll give you – well, it all depends.'

An office cleaner employed in the Ministry of War in Paris was fined the equivalent of £500 and sent to prison for ten years when it was discovered that she had been sealing her pots of home-made jam with top-secret military documents.

Twelve good men and true

Jury. A number of persons appointed by a court to assist the attorney in preventing Law from degenerating into Justice.

Ambrose Bierce

We're all liable to be called for jury service at some time in our lives, provided we're not certified lunatics or barred for other reasons. So you'd think there wouldn't be much of a problem in empanelling a jury. Yet it's surprising how long this process can take. Forty years ago the selection of an American jury took nearly 2½ months, required the summoning of 10,000 'veniremen', the examination of almost 5,000 'talesmen' and the expenditure of the best part of $50,000.

The character of a jury must be foremost in every defendant's mind before he first sets eyes on them at the start of a trial. This certainly preoccupied a man charged in the last century with abducting a woman from her home in London and 'defiling' her in Oxford. As a footnote an account of the case explains, 'Previous to the trial of this case, the counsel for the prisoner, at his request, attended him in prison, when he told them that he had only one suggestion to make, leaving his defence, in other respects, entirely to them; he suggested that in such a case, he had most to fear from passionless, pale, and Cassius-looking

110

jurymen, and therefore he wished them to challenge every jur-yman who had not a red face.'

At the start of a trial in which Abraham Lincoln was appearing for the defence his opposing counsel objected to the presence of one of the jurors because he knew Lincoln, and this could be taken as a reflection on a lawyer's honour. His objection was overruled by Judge Davis. Then came Lincoln's turn to study the jury, two or three of whom, he discovered, knew the prose-cuting counsel. He said as much to the judge who replied, 'Now Mr Lincoln, you are wasting time. The mere fact that a juror knows your opponent does not disqualify him.'

'No, your Honour,' replied Lincoln, 'but I am afraid some of the gentlemen may not know him which would place me at a disadvantage.'

'Do you know anything about this case?' another American juror was asked.

'No.'

'Have you heard anything about it?'

'No.'

'Have you read anything about it?'

'No. I can't read.'

'Have you formed any opinion about the case?'

'What case?'

'Accepted.'

An American railway engineer called to serve on a Federal grand jury asked the judge to excuse him, saying, 'We are very busy at present and I ought to be there.'

'So you are one of those men who think the railroad couldn't get along without you,' answered the judge.

'No, your Honour, that's where you're wrong. I know it could get along without me, but I don't want it to find out.'

'Excused,' said the judge.

Before the start of a trial Baron Alderson dismissed one juryman who admitted he was deaf, saying, 'Please leave the box before the trial begins. It is necessary that the jury should hear both sides.'

Exercising his right to challenge a jury, an Irish defendant in a Waterford court objected to one upright member and had him set aside. When he was later asked why he picked on that particular juryman, the defendant replied, 'Well, you see, it's like this. He's one of those men who would be influenced by the evidence.'

A judge in Santa Cruz, California, dismissed a prospective juror from serving in a case he was about to try, commenting, 'This woman is my wife. She never pays any attention to what I say at home and I have no reason to believe that her behaviour in court would be any different.'

'No one has ever yet been able to find a way of depriving a British jury of its privilege of returning a perverse verdict,' said Lord Chief Justice Goddard in 1955. No matter what verdict it returns a jury is immune from punishment by the judge, should he hold a different opinion. This protection is enshrined in a famous verdict dating from the end of the seventeenth century, delivered by Judge Vaughan.

> I would know whether anything be more common, than for two men students, barristers, or judges, to deduce contrary and opposite conclusions out of the same case in law. And is there any difference that two men should infer distinct conclusions from the same testimony? Is anything more known than that the same author, and place in that author, is forcibly urged to maintain contrary conclusions, and the decision hard, which is the right? Is anything more frequent in the controversies of religion, than to press the same text for opposite tenets? How then comes it to pass that two persons may not apprehend with reason and honesty, what a witness, or many, say, to prove in the understanding of one plainly one thing, but in the apprehension of the other, clearly the contrary thing: must therefore one of these merit fine and imprisonment, because he doth that which he cannot otherside do, preserving his oath and integrity? And this often is the case of the judge and jury.

Exactly.

Mr Justice Maule had this to say to a prisoner inexplicably found guilty by a jury, 'Prisoner at the bar, your counsel thinks you innocent, I think you innocent, but a jury of your own countrymen, in the exercise of such common sense as they possess, which does not appear to be much, have found you guilty, and it remains that I should pass upon you sentence of the law. That sentence is that you be kept in imprisonment for one day, and as that day was yesterday, you may go about your business.'

The jury was out for many hours deliberating the fate of a young man charged with the savage murder of both his parents. The prosecution case had been strong and it appeared to everyone else in the court that he was quite clearly guilty. In the end the judge recalled the jury and asked if he could help them reach a decision. They declined this, saying that they understood the case well enough. The deliberations continued until they finally filed back into the court and delivered the astonishing verdict of 'not guilty'. The court was stunned and the judge so appalled that, quite forgetting himself, asked the foreman how they could possibly have come to such a conclusion, when they knew the prisoner was guilty and should by rights hang.

'That's just it, my Lord,' replied the foreman. 'I assure you we had no doubt about the prisoner's guilt, but we thought there had been deaths enough in the family lately, and so gave him the benefit of the doubt.'

Charles Bowen was making his final address to a jury in an open-and-shut case of burglary and decided to exercise the strength of his prosecution to indulge in a little irony at the expense of the defence. 'If you believe, gentlemen, that the prisoner considered the housetops the proper place for an evening stroll, and by pure accident he happened to have about him the necessary tools of a housebreaker, with no dishonest intention of employing them, you will of course acquit him.'

Unfortunately for Bowen the jury were so overawed by him that they failed to register his innuendo and did exactly as he directed.

An Irish jury is recorded to have returned the verdict, 'We find the man who stole the mare not guilty.'

Daniel O'Connor was defending a man in another Irish court against a charge of murder when the 'corpse' wandered into the courtroom, to general excitement. When order had returned the judge instructed the jury to give the inevitable verdict. However, to everyone's amazement, except theirs, the foreman stood up and declared the defendant 'guilty'.

'But the alleged murdered man is here alive,' roared the judge in disbelief.

'That may be so,' replied the foreman, 'but all I know is that the prisoner stole my brown mare.'

A case of petty larceny that came before a Derbyshire court ended in an acquittal and a recommendation from the jury to the judge that he should tell the defendant 'not to do it again'.

When their turn came to give their verdict the foreman of a Merionethshire jury told the judge, 'My Lord, we do not know who is plaintiff or who is defendant, but we find for whoever is Mr Jones's man.' The Mr Jones in question was a popular local MP and barrister.

Mr Justice Jelf spent several hours carefully summing-up all the issues in a complicated case before leaving the jury to arrive at their verdict. They spent half a day mulling it over but still couldn't come to a decision, so his Lordship called them back and asked what the matter was.

'Only one thing, my Lord,' said the foreman. 'We just want to know what this case is all about.'

A coroner's jury in America were just as baffled about the cause of death in a case they were considering. In the end they returned the only verdict that truly reflected their dilemma, 'An act of God under very suspicious circumstances.'

In the middle of a case tried at York before Mr Justice Gould one of the jurymen went missing. His absence was only noted by the judge some time later and, stopping the proceedings, he asked where the juryman was.

'Please you, my Lord,' said one of the others, 'he's gone away about some business, but he's left his verdict with me.'

At the end of a murder trial a jury retired to consider its verdict with two clear issues in mind: either the deceased had been killed by a hit or he had died as a result of a fall. They were out for some time and when the foreman delivered the verdict to the judge, they were the only ones satisfied with the result.

'We find the deceased died from a blow,' the foreman told the court. 'If the prisoner administered the blow, it was wilful murder. If it was the doorstep, it was manslaughter.'

An American judge who tired of waiting for a jury to return its verdict summarily announced, 'I hereby discharge this jury.'

'You can't do that,' complained one of the twelve.

'And why can't I?' enquired the judge.

'Because you didn't hire me. I'm working for that man,' he exclaimed, pointing at the defence lawyer.

One juror was asked at the end of a week-long trial, 'You must have listened to so much law in the past week that you are almost a lawyer yourself now?'

'You bet,' he replied. 'I'm so full of law that it's going to be difficult to keep from cheating folks after I get back in business.'

A British jury listened carefully to the explanation of the rules of insanity and promptly returned the verdict, 'We are all of one mind – insane.'

In the past it wasn't unknown for juries to be locked away without light, warmth or sustenance until they reached their verdict, and Mr Justice Maule presided once over a trial in which the jury had been so confined in the hope that they would soon reach a satisfactory conclusion. While the court was waiting for their return the bailiff told the judge, whose own taste for port was well known, that one of the jurors was ill and was desperate for a glass of water. 'Let me see,' said Maule, 'water isn't fire, it isn't food, and it certainly isn't drink. Yes, he may have it.'

The great strength of a jury, in spite of the many criticisms laid against the system, is that it does bring a breath of down-to-earth common sense into a courtroom which can very easily become stuffy with the heavy legal arguments and tricks employed by the professionals. The barrister, defending two men from the East End of London who had been charged with being found in possession of burglary tools in the heart of the countryside in the small hours of one morning, was at pains to impress his clients' case on the jury in his final address. The men were not potential housebreakers, he stressed, they were keen ornithologists. This explained, he said why they had finally been caught by the police in the middle of a marsh. They hadn't been running away. They had been trying to find partridges' eggs. Their counsel made great play of this, reminding the jury that one of the accused kept canaries at home that sat on top of the eggs he collected, and speaking up on behalf of honest birdwatchers hounded by the police when they went about their innocent study. His speech had been going rather well when one of the jurymen interrupted and asked if he could put a question. 'Please do,' said the counsel secretly furious, but obliged by law to allow it.

'D'you mind telling me how canaries sit on partridges' eggs?' asked the juror, effectively shattering the defence case.

Judges too can be brought down to earth when they get too carried away for a jury's liking. Sergeant Adams was presiding over a case of nuisance at the Middlesex Sessions and decided to enlarge on the definition of the offence during his summing-up. This was both lengthy and unnecessary with the result that when he finished, and commented, 'I will retire while you are deliberating your verdict, which requires consideration; but I hope you understand the various points I have submitted to you?' the foreman answered, 'Oh yes, my Lord; we are all agreed that we never before knew what a nuisance was until we heard your Lordship's summing-up.'

A recent trial for attempted murder held in a Manitoba court began inauspiciously and ended abruptly even before the charge had been read out. At the swearing in of the jury one of the twelve men asked the judge to speak up because he was very deaf. Further enquiries revealed that another juryman was stone deaf and thought he was about to hear a divorce case. Three others couldn't understand a word of English and another had only come to the court to apply for a gun licence.

Dusty purlieus of the law

*If you think that you can think about a thing, inextricably attached to
something else, without thinking of the thing it is attached to, then you
have a legal mind.*

Thomas Reed Powell

'The life of the law,' said that great American judge, Oliver
Wendell Holmes, 'has not been logic; it has been experience.'
This perhaps goes some way towards explaining the origin of
the many bizarre pieces of legislation that have found their way
on to the world's statute books into whose murky depths they
have sunk, there to remain hidden and forgotten for the most
part, only to raise their heads in later times like creatures from a
bygone age.

In Iraq it's illegal to eat snakes on a Sunday. Camels are
protected from hunters in the State of Arizona, though to ride
one down the street in Vancouver, British Columbia, is likely to
put you at odds with the Mounties. It's not so long ago that a ban
existed in St James's and Green Park on pushing bathchairs
three abreast and, if my memory serves me correctly, as recently
as 1819 the death penalty was still in force for anyone attempting to impersonate a Chelsea pensioner; making a false entry in
the books of the Bank of England, or damaging Westminster
Bridge. (As far as I know you can still be sent to the hangman for
piracy with violence or high treason.)

Combing through legal codes can be an entertaining if not
always reassuring experience. Presumably every law must have

been drafted by someone with a certain amount of grey matter, though it is often questionable what use they put it to. Why it should be illegal to sell anti-freeze to Indians in Quebec, to hang male and female underwear on the same washing-line in Minnesota, or to drink water in the beer parlours of Saskatchewan is beyond my understanding. But then as Edward Biggon observed, 'The laws of a nation form the most instructive portion of its history,' and history, as Henry Ford reminded us, 'is more or less bunk'.

From the Cyprus Act 1960:
An order in Council under this section may provide either that all the provisions of section three of this Act and of the Schedule thereto (except in so far as they relate to the areas mentioned in subsection (1) of section two of this Act) shall cease to have effect or that those provisions shall continue in force to such extent and subject to such modifications as may be specified in the Order, may make such adaptations or modifications of any Act (other than this Act) in force at the making of the Order or passed before then and coming into force thereafter, or any instrument having effect under any such Act, as appear to Her Majesty in Council expedient for the purposes or in consequence of the Order, and may contain incidental, consequential and supplemental provisions.

From the Revised Statutes of Kansas, 1923, section 21-2426:
It shall be unlawful for any person to exhibit in a public way within the State of Kansas, any sort of an exhibition that consists of eating or pretending to eat of snakes, lizards, scorpions, centipedes, tarantulas, or other reptiles.

Dusty purlieus of the law

Ordinance No. 75169 of the city of Los Angeles, California:
It shall be unlawful for any person to have, keep or maintain, or cause to permit to be had, kept or maintained or to have in possession or under control within the City of Los Angeles, any elephant, bear, hippopotamus, rhinoceros, lion, tiger, leopard, wolf, or any poisonous reptile of any kind, without first applying to and receiving permission from the Board of Police Commissioners a permit to do so.

From an Indian newspaper report:
A notification from the Commissioner of Police today said that discharge or firing of certain varieties of crackers like atom bomb and rocket which produce a disturbing noise in or near any public place, particularly within a radius of half a mile from hospitals and nursing homes, had also been prohibited.

Section 338 of the Statutes of El Paso, Texas:
Churches and Hotels and All Public Places of Resort. In and at all public places of resort and amusement, such as churches or hotels or halls of assembly, or stores or markets or banking-rooms or railroad depots or waiting stations or saloons, shall be required at the expense of the owners or persons in charge of same, or under whose control or care the same are, to be provided with spittoons of a kind and number to efficiently contain expectorations into them...

During the reign of King Charles II a man named Walcott, one of the conspirators in the Rye House Plot, was executed in 1683 for his part in the treason. Twelve years after his death the verdict was reversed and a writ of error was moved because in the original sentence it had not been stated that his entrails should be burnt 'while he was still alive'.

From section 36 (10) 1951 Finance Act:
. . . And a body corporate shall not be deemed for the purposes of this section to cease to be resident in the United Kingdom by reason only that it ceases to exist.

Buying a mousetrap in the State of Colorado is no easy business. Successful candidates must first produce a small-game licence issued by the police authorities, according to state legislation.

From a law report:
Sacrificing accuracy somewhat recklessly for the sake of brevity, I am tempted to say that the object of the action is to determine which of these two bodies, if either, is the other, and, if not, whether either, and if so which, is another corporate body of the same name, or if not in fact such third body, is identical with it.

From Act 64 of the State of Louisiana, 1914:
No woman may wear hatpins which protrude from the crown of the hat more than ½ inch. In case such a pin is worn longer than ½ inch from the crown of the hat, it is to be protected by a shield or sheath.

From the National Insurance Bill, 1959:
For the purpose of this part of the schedule a person over

pensionable age, not being an insured person, shall be treated as an employed person if he would be an insured person were he under pensionable age and would be an employed person were he an insured person.

From a US press release:
The Federal Communications Commission had advised that there is nothing in the law to prevent two licensed amateur radio stations being utilized to consummate a wedding ceremony between a couple separated by the Pacific Ocean.

Unexpected problems arose when it was finally decided to turn the Royal Navy's last wartime destroyer, HMS *Cavalier*, into a museum at Southampton. The chairman of the trust set up to administer this fine example of service history, Vice-Admiral Sir Ian McIntosh, discovered that he needed permission from the Home Office to have the ship towed from Chatham to her final destination. This peculiar state of affairs arose because all the guns aboard the ship were still in working order. The problem was fortunately soon overcome in the best traditions of English law. Sir Ian was granted a firearms certificate.

Section 1 of the Tennessee Act, incorporating the town of Ripley, Lauderdale County, Tennessee:
Be it enacted by the General Assembly of the State of Tennessee, that . . . the boundaries of said town of Ripley shall be as follows: Beginning at a stake in the west boundary line of the present limits of the old corporation ... thence North eighty-five degrees and East to a blackgum marked with a cross and with

mistletoe in the top, and with a bluebird sitting on a limb which tree is a short distance East of Ed Johnson's horse lot . . .

From section 1 of Ordinance No. 32928 of Portland, Oregon:
Bathing without Suitable Dress. It shall be unlawful to bathe in the waters of the Willamette River, or in the waters of any lake, slough or creek within the corporate limits of the City of Portland between the hours of six o'clock a.m. and half-past eight p.m. without wearing a suitable dress, which shall cover the body from the neck to the knees, and no person while so attired in said bathing suit or otherwise, shall unnecessarily expose himself to the public view . . .

A public-spirited legislator in Texas took a dim view of his colleagues' cursory perusal of the bills that passed through their assembly. In 1967 the situation had become so intolerable that he literally took the law into his own hands and introduced a bill commending 'Mr Albert DeSalvo for his outstanding work in population control'. The bill was passed unanimously even though Mr DeSalvo was currently on trial, charged with murdering 13 women, under his more lurid *alter ego* 'The Boston Strangler'.

From the Local Government Act 1966, the Resources Element Schedule 1, Part II:
(1) For the purposes of this part of the Schedule, the standard penny rate product for an area for any year is the sum which bears to the product of a rate of one penny in the pound for that year for the whole of England and Wales the same proportion as the population of the area bears to the population of England and Wales; but in ascertaining the standard penny rate product

for a county or county borough the population of any county in the case of which the ratio of the population to the road-mileage of the county is less than seventy shall be increased by one-half of the additional population needed in order that the population divided by the road-mileage should be seventy.

(2) In this paragraph 'population' means estimated population.

From a transportation law in the State of Kansas:
When two trains approach each other at a crossing, they shall both stop, and neither shall start up until the other has gone.

Section 45 of Chapter 5 of the Code of the City of Columbia, Tennessee:
It shall be unlawful for three or more persons to assemble upon any of the sidewalks of this corporation, so as to impede the free passage of persons upon the sidewalk.

A piece of nutty British law:
In the Nuts (unground) (other than ground nuts) Order, the expression nuts shall have reference to such nuts, other than ground nuts, as would but for this amending Order not qualify as nuts (unground) (other than ground nuts) by reason of their being nuts (unground).

The Landlord and Tenant Act, 1927, was the subject of a learned legal treatise published in 1931. For those who depended on the *Irish Law Times* to bring this work to their notice a long wait ensued. It wasn't until 1942 in fact that that esteemed publication finally brought out a review introduced with the disarming comment that it regretted 'that we had not an earlier opportunity to draw our readers' attention to this work'.

An ordinance passed in the city of Abilene, Texas:
It shall be unlawful for any person to idle or loiter on any street or thoroughfare, sidewalk, or alley, or in any store, theater, motor car, motion picture show, business house, or in the entrance or doorway of any place within the corporate limits of the city of Abilene for the purpose of plying the avocation of flirt or masher.

It shall further be unlawful for any man to stare at or make googoo eyes at, or in any other manner look at or make remarks to or concerning, or cough or whistle at, or do any other act to attract the attention of any woman upon or travelling along any of the sidewalks, streets, public ways of the city of Abilene with an intent or in a manner calculated to annoy such woman.

An ordinance passed in 1910 in Waterloo, Nebraska:
It shall be illegal for any barber in this town to eat onions between 7 a.m. and 7 p.m.

Section 5539, 1928 Code of Alabama:
... any person who engages in domino playing on Sunday ... must be fined.

In an effort to combat the growing abuse of public libraries the council of Widnes, Lancashire, introduced stiff penalties for offenders. Browsers found resting on the floor became liable to a fine of £5 as did those who made a habit of falling asleep in the reading rooms. A library official was at pains to point out that those who dropped off by accident and short-sighted readers who had to lie down to read titles on the bottom shelves would not be penalized under the new by-laws.

From a US patent for removing casings from sausages and the like:
In a sausage-skinning machine, means for rotating a sausage about its longitudinal axis, means for holding a part of the skin against rotative movement with the sausage to cause said skin to be torn off said sausage circumferentially, and means for simultaneously moving said sausage endwise with respect to said holding means, said rotating, holding and moving means being operatively related to one another to cause said skin to be torn off and stripped from the sausage helically.

Ordinance 381 from Wichita, Kansas:
That it shall be unlawful or any person to throw upon or against another person in the city of Wichita, any confetti or similar preparation or to throw same about in any street or public building or place in said city. It is further made unlawful for any person to throw as aforesaid any flour, talcum powder, rice or other substance or preparations for the purpose of annoying or harassing others.

So firmly enshrined in the American constitution is the right to bear arms that the police of Ecorse, Michigan, were unable to find any precedent to prevent them from issuing a gun licence to a blind man.

According to a by-law in Shawnee, Oklahoma, a nuisance can be said to occur:

> When three or more dogs congregate on any private property without the consent of the owner or occupant and annoy such owners or occupants ...

Section 9998 of the North Dakota Compiled Laws, 1913:
Every person who offers to sell any beef and fails to exhibit to the purchaser on demand the hide of the animal to be sold, and does not keep such hide for ten days after the sale, at his place of residence, or refuses to allow the same to be inspected by any person is punishable ...

From the Ohio General Code, Title II, Ch.20, p.1590, Sec.6281:
A person assaulted and lynched by a mob may recover from the county in which such assault is made, a sum not exceeding five hundred dollars.

Among the charges heard at the first hearing of the first juvenile court was that of 'Shouting celery in the street'.

Until 1859 it was illegal *not* to celebrate the date of Guy Fawkes's arrest in England!

From the New York statute books – Sanitary Code, Section 9, Article 2:
If you have a dead horse, place it in the street at once with tag

giving name and address; if not removed at twilight, put lights around properly protected carcass till called for.

An ordinance passed in Alderson, West Virginia, states: 'No lions shall be allowed to run wild on the streets of this city.'

The following amendment was made to the Air Force Act:
Section 138, Para. (8), line 4. Delete 'bastard' and substitute 'illegitimate'.

Amending legislation may strike the layman as being tediously pedantic. In cases where the draftsman has taken his task with less than the usual scrupulous accuracy, however, calamity has often followed. Take for example the case of the bill that provided for a certain offence to be punishable by a fine. This was later upgraded and the penalty became transportation. The old bill was altered, but only in part. After stating the new sanction, it continued 'and that upon conviction one-half thereof should go to the King and one-half to the informer'!

An Act of Parliament that covered the rebuilding of Chelmsford prison also came unstuck at the drafting stage. One section of the bill set out that the new prison was to be constructed from materials obtained from the dismantling of the old one; though according to a later section the prisoners were to remain housed in the old prison until the new one was built.

Even the best intentioned legislation does not always have a smooth ride. The mayor of the small Brazilian town Angra Dos Reis threw himself into a municipal clean-up campaign and decreed that the principal malefactors, the dozens of mules that passed through the town each day, had in future to wear nappies. This innocent attempt to drag Angra Dos Reis out of the Middle Ages resulted in an uproar. Local mule owners said they were faced with bankruptcy and the chief of police handed in his badge. As far as he was concerned the law was impossible to enforce. The mules won the day.

A British farmer ground down by the tax system hit on a novel way to make the law work to his benefit for once. While he was away on his honeymoon he arranged for his hens to feed on the rice thrown over him and his bride at the church gate. This simple ploy then enabled him to offset all his wedding expenses against tax. Thanks to the hens they became part of the running costs of his farm.

From ordinance No. 16 of Columbus, Montana:
... any person who shall not lift his hat to the Mayor as he passes on the street, will be guilty of a misdemeanour.

(This strikes a different chord to a more recent case in Teesside when a local man was taken in front of the bench for making a two-fingered gesture at a High Court judge he'd seen in the street. The man was acquitted when he explained that he'd mistaken the judge for the mayor!)

Federation Rules Decision, Grau *v.* Proctor & Gamble Co., *United States District Court, MD Alabama ND:*
On January 8, 1963, the official court reporter for this district

filed with the Clerk of this Court a certified transcript of the proceedings of this case. Subsequent to the filing of the original certified transcript by the court reporter, the defendants, now the appellees, asked this Court to strike and eliminate certain portions thereof. The exact portions of the record, which this Court is asked to strike are as follows:

Page 24: *Mr Garrett:* Ha, ha, ha, ha.

* * * * * * * * *

Mr Garrett: Ha, ha, ha, ha.

Page 42: *Q (Mr Garrett):* Ha, ha, ha, ha.

* * * * * * * * *

Q (Mr Garrett): Ha, ha, ha.

Page 74: *Q (Mr Garrett):* Ha, ha.

Page 82: *Mr Garrett:* Ha, ha, ha.

Page 105: *Mr Garrett:* Ha, ha, ha, ha.

Juror: Ha, ha, ha.

In asking this Court to edit the record and strike the above portions, the appellees state 'that although Mr Garrett and the juror may have made some sound at such times, that it was an inadvertent mannerism, such as a person coughing, clearing his throat or otherwise inadvertently making a sound'. The appellees contend that the inclusion of the above portions of the proceedings merely serve to clutter unduly the record on appeal in this case. The plaintiff, now the appellent, formally objects to altering or changing the official transcript.

From section 74, California State Housing Act:
No horse, cow, calf, swine, sheep, goat, rabbit, mule or other animal, chicken, pigeon, goose, duck or other poultry shall be kept in any apartment house or hotel or any part thereof.

In the days when the delights of Highland cuisine were still a novelty in Latin America, a haggis was once admitted duty-free by customs officials in São Paulo, Brazil. After consulting an analytical chemist they classified the haggis as 'Unscheduled horticulture fertilizer'.

Shakespeare may remind us in one of his most celebrated lines that '... that which we call a rose/ By any other name would smell as sweet' but as far as the law is concerned this isn't necessarily the case. For one who practised a profession notorious for its pedantry Lord Darling once gave an unusually enlightened exposition of what he termed the 'many erroneous terms consecrated by common use':

> One which has been mentioned in the course of the argument, a glaring instance is the term 'Bombay ducks' as applied to an Indian fish, and it is agreed that if anybody ordered Bombay ducks and somebody supplied him with ducks from Bombay, the contract to supply Bombay ducks would not be fulfilled. Another obvious instance is Eau de Cologne. Whatever Eau de Cologne may be, as to which I now nothing, it certainly is not water from the Rhine. If Eau de Cologne were ordered and you simply supplied a gallon of water from Cologne that would not fulfil the contract. Another instance where anybody would understand what was meant is if you speak of Roman pearls. They are not pearls with which any oyster has had anything to do, nor do I know that they are Roman. They indicate something that is probably neither Roman nor a pearl, just as it was said by a well-known historian that the Holy Roman Empire had for its chief characteristic that it was neither holy nor Roman nor an empire. One other instance occurs to me of a term consecrated, if I may say so, by common usage which does not indicate the true fact, and that is when people speak as they commonly do of the judicial ermine, meaning merely any white fur when worn by a judge. These expressions have become conventional terms and are, I think, instances of a trade description lawfully and generally applied.

As a coda it's worth considering the lengths to which some litigants will go in the pursuit of justice. One notorious British case started life in the Archdeacon's Court in Totnes, from where it went to appeal in three higher courts until it was finally settled. The point at issue had been which of the two parties had the right of hanging his hat on a particular peg.

Yet even this is eclipsed by a case reported from India where a court in Poona finally concluded a lawsuit in the spring of 1966 after it had been contested for 761 years. The case had received its first airing in 1205, but the descendants of the plaintiff refused to let the matter die until they had received favourable judgement. By the court's final decision they eventually gained precedence at religious festivals and the right to preside over public functions.

Perhaps they'd have fared better if they had taken a leaf out of Cornelius Vanderbilt's book when he wrote to an associate who had not behaved ethically in a deal:

> You have undertaken to cheat me. I will not sue you because the law takes too long. I will ruin you.

Paragraph 187 of Penal Code 6260, California State Vehicle Act, Chapter XVIII:
It is a misdemeanour to shoot at any kind of game bird or mammal except a whale, from an automobile or airplane.

For better for worse

I suppose it is a very pleasant thing to commit adultery but it becomes rather monotonous to listen to other people having done it, hour after hour and day after day.

Mr Justice Swift

'Ignorance of the law,' wrote John Selden, 'excuses no man', not that that has ever prevented defendants from trying their luck, notably, it would seem, in affairs of the heart and other amorous adventures. Mr Justice Swift may have learned much during his time in the Divorce Court but even he would have been amazed at some of the definitions of adultery trotted out by hopeful co-respondents, definitions like: 'I thought it meant getting a girl into trouble'; 'I thought it meant drinking with men in public houses'; 'I did not think it was adultery during the daytime'; and 'Adultery is having sexual connexion with a woman not your wife, who is not over fifty years of age; and it is not adultery if she is over fifty.'

Divorce today is a relatively simple process compared with the law as it stood in the past. The procedure was once long-winded and costly; it even required a special Act of Parliament. The story is told of one enterprising Town Clerk, clearly one of the few to understand the workings of the law as it then was, who succeeded in obtaining a divorce at very little personal expense. After enduring years of misery with his better half he saw escape in a municipal Waterworks Bill. As the civil officer responsible for drafting the bill he was able to turn it to his own advantage and throughout the bill's passage no one noticed his unusual entry in clause 64. Hidden among the technical description was the innocent phrase on which his future happiness depended, '. . . and the Town Clerk's marriage is hereby dissolved'. The Royal Assent was given to the bill. The town got its new water supply and the Town Clerk became a free man. Not everyone was so lucky.

The iniquities of the old divorce laws were apparent even to those who made their living out of them. Among the fiercest critics and advocates for reform was Mr Justice Maule who took the opportunity to issue a blistering attack in one famous summing up at the end of a trial for bigamy:

Clerk of Assize: What have you to say that judgement should not be passed upon you according to the law?
Prisoner: Well, my Lord, my wife took up with a hawker and ran away five years ago; and I have never seen her since, so I married this other woman last winter.
Mr Justice Maule: Prisoner at the Bar, I will tell you what you ought to have done, and if you say you did not know, I will tell you that the Law conclusively presumes that you did. You ought to have instructed your attorney to bring an action against the hawker for criminal conversation with your wife. That would have cost you about £100. When you had recovered substantial damages against the hawker, you would have instructed your attorney to sue in the ecclesiastical courts for a divorce *a mensa et toro*. That would have cost you £200 or £300 more. When you had obtained a divorce *a mensa et toro*, you would have had to appear by counsel before the House of Lords for a divorce *a vinculo matrimonii*. The Bill might have been opposed in all its stages in both Houses of Parliament, and altogether you would have had to spend about £1,000 or £1,200. You will probably tell me that you never had 1,000 farthings of your own in the world, but, prisoner, that makes no difference. Sitting here as a British

judge, it is my duty to tell you that this is not a country in which there is one law for the rich and another for the poor.

Even after reforms were introduced divorce was still a lucrative occupation for lawyers, though along with other enterprises this took a down-turn during the war. According to *Reynolds News*:

> West End solicitors, who before the war netted five-figure incomes from divorce cases, have been heavily hit by the black-out. In the winter months, at any rate, private inquiry agents are helpless. Adultery cannot be proved because identification is impossible in the pitch dark.

In an effort to combat the promiscuity of the swinging sixties and permissive seventies the House in Harrisburg, Pennsylvania voted by 180 to 69 to outlaw pre-marital and extra-marital sex in the state.

Relationships in any eternal triangle are never easy and in the case of one Nottinghamshire threesome they can't have been improved when the deserted husband moved in as lodger with his estranged wife and her lover. Even then they might have been able to get along had the lover pulled his weight. As it was the case eventually ended up in court where the husband rebuked the other man for failing to do his share of the housework.

After 17 years of marriage a mother of three finally decided that she could take no more. Her husband was in the garden at the time and she called out to him, 'I am getting a divorce.' As evidence of the irretrievable breakdown of the marriage the Family Division of the High Court was told that the man's only reply was, 'If I do not get these tomato plants in soon they will die.'

A wife who petitioned for a decree of nullity on the claim that her husband was impotent had this rejected by the court as a result of the insubstantial evidence of the medical inspectors who had made an intimate examination of that part of her husband's anatomy said to be at fault. In the judge's own carefully chosen words, 'They could only say it appeared soft and small which does not always continue.'

In 1947 divorce proceedings laid before the court in West Surrey by an unhappy husband was later withdrawn 'in case his wife got to hear about it'.

The French legal system recognizes a *crime passionnel*, one caused by sexual passion, and that has often let otherwise guilty husbands off the hook. If precedence carries the same weight in France as it does in Britain, French husbands may have a *crime gastronomique* to fall back on as well. In 1973 a Parisian admitted killing his first wife because she always undercooked his steak and his second wife, twelve years later, because she went to the other extreme and always served it *bien cuit*. After taking into account all the evidence the judge cleared him of murder and imposed a sentence of eight years for manslaughter, explaining, 'The quality of the cooking is an important part of marriage.'

It is not uncommon for one partner in a marriage to be keen to get a divorce while the other is dead against it. One extreme case was brought before a court in which the husband refused to agree to a separation so stubbornly that three male accomplices of his wife tried to drag him into bed with a strange woman, in order to photograph him committing 'adultery'. The husband managed to break the camera and escape, and then joined the army to avoid a repetition of the incident.

Mr Justice Langton was well known for his summings-up of divorce cases brought before him. Here he is describing the parties in a case where a couple remarried after a previous divorce, brought about by the husband's adultery, only to seek a second divorce ten years later, in which both of them filed petitions:

> Mr Spence is a man whose character it is not at all difficult to read. In the course of the argument, I pointed out more than once that he had impressed me as a perfectly honest man . . . He is, however, a man of such a high temper and such intensity of conviction that it is almost impossible for him to state any case, whether his own or someone else's, dispassionately or fairly. To take a few instances which remain in my memory, he is obviously a man of most violent political views. Only with difficulty did I succeed in preventing him from launching upon a diatribe against a distinguished ex-Cabinet minister who has political connections with Leamington. In passing allusions to his wife, he described her as having a genius for nagging, and the worst sense of humour in the world, and he is obviously ready to believe that in meanness, avarice, and ingratitude she is without rival, and beyond compare . . . By a great effort of self-control, Mr Spence managed to restrain his irascibility during a great portion of his sojourn in the witness-box, but towards the end his impatience so frequently got the better of him that I was obliged to intervene to save cross-examining counsel from the full consequences of his wrath.

Of the wife he said:

140

For my part, I am not afraid to go further, and to express the view that she is a woman of exceptional obstinacy and determination. While listening to her evidence, I endeavoured not to lose sight of the fact that her husband, far older than herself, had wronged her seriously as a young woman, and, after I had made Mr Spence's acquaintance, and had heard and seen him for four hours in the witness-box, I was well able to believe that he was a most difficult man with whom to live. Bearing all this in mind, and making the greatest allowances for Mrs Spence, I am satisfied that she was hard and unsympathetic, and went to work in the worst possible way to deal with a spirited and choleric husband who was not without great qualities of mind and heart.

Turning finally to the nature of their physical conflict, he commented:

In the course of these undignified but not very serious combats, both received physical injuries which have, I am afraid, left unforgettable mental scars. Mr Spence, who, it will be remembered, was a man nearing seventy years of age at the time, and in anything but continuously robust health at the period, tells me that he has had dressed by a doctor wounds inflicted by his wife through the medium of the fire-irons. Mrs Spence, on the other hand, complains of a series of acts which she has sought to elevate to the height of legal cruelty, but which, when sifted, do not amount to anything more than her natural portion of the damage likely to accrue from a rough-and-tumble with a small, much older, but very determined husband.

Taking all the factors into consideration he concluded:

Their married life came to shipwreck the second time, neither on account of any cruelty on the part of Mr Spence, nor, as was further suggested against him, on account of his attentions to other women, but solely because two people of inflexible will were daily pitting themselves against each other in every small rub of married life, without any particle of the softening influence of mutual affection and esteem.

During a divorce case presided over by Mr Justice Swift the counsel for the respondent was at pains to stress his client's fine war record. After hearing at some length of the man's military prowess the judge raised a finger of reproval and remarked: 'In my view, there is no consistency between gallantry on the battle-field and gallantry in the boudoir.'

Sir Ellis Hume-Williams once remarked to a jury in a divorce action:

> If ladies should ever lose their habit of keeping diaries, it would destroy one of the few remaining safeguards for the purity of English domestic life.

An argument that developed in a courtroom in Jacksonville, Florida, led to unexpected consequences when both parties in a legal separation drew guns and began shooting it out from opposite sides of the judge's chamber. A witness in an adjoining room borrowed a pistol from the judge to whom he was giving evidence, dashed into the scene of the gunfight and shot both husband and wife dead.

Twenty years ago Mr Justice Laughton ruled in a case of wife-beating that a little thumping on a Saturday night might not constitute cruelty in some parts of England (he was speaking in Sheffield) but that in Cheltenham there would be no doubt that it was an act of cruelty. The social background had to be taken into consideration he said.

The course of true love never did run smooth as Carlisle magis-trates learned from a husband who appeared before them on a charge of assaulting his wife. During cross-examination the man admitted to having stripped her, stuffed some of her clothes in her mouth, tied her hands behind her back and hit her. He went on to explain that he had been making a desperate attempt to show that their marriage was not over.

Another magistrate presiding over a case of wife-beating observed that at times there was nothing against a man hitting his wife; it was sanctioned by the Bible after all. He went on to emphasize that action like this should be considered as an action of love, not one of anger. In the circumstances of the case before him he regretted that the husband had chosen to use an iron bar and not a reasonably-sized stick.

Passing judgement in the Divorce Court Mr Justice Karminski remarked that a wife who threw 'almost every form of domestic utensil' at her husband could not be considered cruel because on almost every occasion she had missed.

Loyal to the end, a Glasgow wife admitted to a court that her husband had burnt her with lighted cigarettes and given her two black eyes. When asked, 'And is that what you regard as a happy marriage?' she answered, 'Oh yes.'

Even the powers of justice were unable to protect one wretched woman who secured a court order forbidding her husband to beat her. She returned home, confident that her life would now show signs of improvement only to have her husband force her to eat the court order before he beat her again. For this misdemeanour he was fined £38.

A former Lord Chancellor, Lord Goddard, once ruled in the Court of Criminal Appeal that divorce, not murder, was the remedy for a man who wished to rid himself of an unfaithful wife.

In the past judges have been careful not to let couples rush too hastily into divorce. On many occasions the grounds presented as evidence have left the judge unconvinced of the validity of the petition. When a 50-year-old wife sought a divorce on the grounds of cruelty she cited among her allegations the fact that her husband had slapped her round the face with a wet fish twenty years earlier. As the judge said, 'If one slap with a wet fish in 40 years of marriage is cruel – and I don't consider that it is – then that cruelty has, in any case, been forgiven.'

The ease with which marriages and divorces can be procured in Reno, Nevada, have occasionally led to both institutions being treated with undue levity. When Mr and Mrs Holt decided to end their life together, Mr Holt took himself off to Reno and filed his divorce suit. Three days later Mrs Holt arrived and they lived together for a further three days before she departed. Some time later, Mrs Holt applied through the courts for alimony. Her husband tried to block this by citing the divorce he had received in Reno. This was met by the reply of condonation, in other words that his behaviour in Reno had demonstrated that he had forgiven Mrs Holt whatever offences had driven him to seek a divorce. The case went to appeal where Judge Hitz again found against Mr Holt, saying, 'Though we have seen much of the liberality of Nevada practice, we assume that even in that forward-looking jurisdiction parties to a cause of divorce may not litigate by day and copulate by night, *inter sese et pendente lite.*'

A similar marital confusion arose between a British couple whose tale of woe finally made its way to the Divorce Court. The wife, it appeared, had confessed adultery with the owner of an ice-cream cart. According to her testimony she repented this folly and wrote a letter to her paramour which her husband delivered in person. The men shook hands and the husband returned with two free cornets. This, she claimed, showed that her husband had forgiven her. Clearly the husband thought otherwise.

Weakness at the eleventh hour cost one German wife her freedom as a Dortmund court discovered when her case was presented. The day before the hearing she had gone to her husband's office to settle a minor issue about their property. During their meeting the husband had argued forcibly against their separation, but the wife, by her own admission, had remained resolute. Therefore it came as an unpleasant surprise to hear her husband exclaim 'It's a lie!' when she told the judge that they had last made love 'at least eighteen months ago'.

'We made love on the floor of my office yesterday morning!' persisted the husband.

'He's the one who is lying,' retorted his wife.

But the husband won the day. 'I can prove it,' he shouted triumphantly. 'I marked her bottom with the office date-stamp.'

A New York man who wrote 'adulteress' on all his divorced wife's alimony cheques was finally ordered to stop this by one of the city's judges when he ruled, 'No woman should be put in the position of publishing libel against herself in order to cash a cheque to which she is entitled.'

A French seaman, Marcel Rivien, won a breach-of-promise suit brought against him by a girl he had agreed to marry on the grounds that he couldn't be expected to marry a girl with twelve tattoos on her chest.

Lord Chief Justice Russell was once asked for the penalty for bigamy to which he replied without hesitation, 'Two mothers-in-law!'

After an Irish court had convicted a Dublin man of bigamy the judge expressed his horror that he could have deceived so many innocent women. 'Please, your lordship,' replied the defendant, 'I was only trying to get a good one.'

Mr Justice Byles, who developed a formidable reputation for his astuteness in cross-examination, once represented a man in a breach-of-promise action in which the plaintiff had given con-clusive proof that his client had agreed to marry her. Much to the plaintiff's dismay Cupid's arrow had struck her betrothed from different quarters and he had plighted his troth with another. The cases looked cut and dried and it only seemed a matter of agreeing the damages, but Byles was not beaten.

'Did he not propose to marry you when his father was dead?' he asked the girl.

'Yes,' she replied.

'Is his father dead?'

'No.'

'That is my case, my lord,' said the triumphant advocate.

'But, brother Byles,' said the judge, 'he has married somebody else!'

'Well, my lord, his wife may die before his father, or afterwards, and he may outlive them both, when it will be time to fulfil the promise.'

On the basis of this submission the defendant won his case.

On a happier note let us round off with a case of breach-of-promise brought by a Miss Week against a Mr Day. Before the action was brought to court the couple made up their differences and announced their intention to marry after all. Frank Lockwood (later Solicitor-General) who had been engaged to represent the plaintiff jotted down the following summary which he passed to the judge for his approval:

'One Day the more, one Week the less,
But we must not complain.
There'll soon be little Days enough
To make a Week again.'

Judge Clothier once presided over an unusual case in the Divorce Court in which a husband was seeking a divorce on the

grounds of his wife's unnatural demands. These were not re-stricted, as one might suppose, to the bedroom, but literally embraced the whole family. After hearing the plaintiff his lordship ruled that the wife had adopted a very unreasonable attitude in insisting that on his return home her husband should first kiss her, then her sister and lastly the cat.

Death where is thy sting?

The art of will-making chiefly consists in baffling the importunity of expectation.

William Hazlitt

The majority of wills are humdrum affairs by solicitors and executed with the minimum of fuss and bother. These tend to be written on paper. There are, however, those refreshing, rare exceptions written on egg-shells, stable-doors, ladders, petticoats, and even on the back of a brass service identity disc, which shine out like beacons to more adventurous spirits to indulge in a final fling of eccentric whimsy before crossing over to the other side.

Wills can be touching, cruel, sentimental, acerbic, vindictive, generous, or anything else that the testator chooses to make them. Yet they all share one thing in common; they represent the last chance that any of us have to make our presence felt in this life, or put another way, the first opportunity we have to make those left behind aware of our existence in the next.

The late Sir William Bagnall, a judge famous for his knowledge of trust and property law, died leaving £96,837 gross, £0.0p net. His widow's only comment was, 'This is not surprising, he was a tax expert and very astute.' On the other hand rock star Janis Joplin left, amongst other things, £2,500 for a farewell party to be held at her favourite local, the Lion's Share, San Anselmo, California.

Philanthropy has often had a part to play in will-making. Take for instance the will of a former Master of the Rolls, Sir Joseph Jekyll, who left his fortune to settle the National Debt. This act of public generosity was met with almost universal ridicule. Lord Mansfield described it as 'a very foolish one. He might as well have attempted to stop the middle arch of Blackfriars bridge with his full-bottomed wig.' Sir Joseph's family succeeded in getting his will set aside on the grounds of imbecility.

Animals have frequently been the beneficiaries of wills. A famous French harpist of the second half of the seventeenth century, one Madame Dupuis, made sure hers were well provided for by including in her will:

> *Item:* I desire my sister, Marie Bluteau, and my niece, Madame Calonge, to look to my cats. If both should survive me, thirty sous a week must be laid out upon them, in order that they may live well.
>
> They are to be served daily, in a clean and proper manner, with two meals of meat soup, the same as we eat ourselves, but it is to be given to them separately in two soup-plates. The bread is not to be cut into the soup, but must be broken into squares about the size of a nut, otherwise they will refuse to eat it. A ration of meat, finely minced, is to be added to it; the whole is then to be mildly seasoned, put into a clean pan, covered close, and carefully simmered before it is dished up. If only one cat should survive, half the sum mentioned will suffice.
>
> Nicole-Page is to take charge of my two cats, and to be very careful of them. Madame Calonge is to visit them three times a week.

Cooking directions (for human consumption) featured in a will made by Maggie Noth of Philadelphia in 1913. One can only hazard a guess what passed through her mind as she was thumbing through her cookery book one day, but under the title *Chili Sauce Without Working* comes:

4 quarts of ripe tomatoes, 4 small onions, 4 green peppers, 2 teacups of sugar, 2 quarts of cider vinegar, 2 ounces ground allspice, 2 ounces cloves, 2 ounces cinnamon, 12 teaspoonfuls salt. Chop tomatoes, onions and peppers fine, add the rest mixed together and bottle cold. Measure tomatoes when peeled. In case I die before my husband I leave everything to him.

The problem of how to make a will when you have nothing to bequeath has been overcome in a number of ingenious ways. An English resident of Calcutta got round the problem like this:

In the name of God, I, Daniel Martinett, of the town of Calcutta . . . make this my last will and testament . . . To avoid Latin phrases, as it is a tongue I am not well versed in, I shall speak plain English. First. In the most submissive manner I recommend my soul to Almighty God.

Secondly. Now as to worldly concerns, In the following manner: As to this fulsome carcase having already seen enough of worldly pomp, I desire nothing relative to it do be done, only its being stowed away in my old green chest, to avoid expense; for as I lived profusely, I die frugally.

Thirdly. The undertaker's fees come to nothing, as I won them from him at a game of billiards in the presence of Mr Thomas Morice and William Perkes, at the same William Perkes' house, in February last. I furthermore request . . . that the Rev. Mr Henry Butler read the prayers which are customary and also preach a funeral sermon . . . but as my finances are low, and cannot conveniently discharge his fees, I hope he will please accept the will for the deed.

Fourthly. To Henry Vansittart, Esq., as an opulent man, I leave the discharge of all sums of money (the whole not exceeding 300 rupees) that I shall stand indebted to indigent persons in the town of Calcutta.

Fifthly. To Mr George Grey, Secretary of the Presidency, I bequeath all my sincerity.

Sixthly. To Mr Simon Drose, Writer to the Secretary's office, all my modesty.

Seventhly. To Mr Henry Higgenson, also of the Secretary's office, all the thoughts I hope I shall die possessed of.

Eighthly. To Thomas Forbes, all the worldly assurance which I had when I had taken a cheerful glass, though in face of doleful cup.

As I have lived the make-game of a modern gentleman, being a butt for envy and a mark for malice, by acting a little out of the common road, though, thank God, never in a base way, I hope I may die in sincere love and charity to all men, forgiving all my persecutors, as I hope for forgiveness from my Creator.

As it lies not in my power to bequeath anything to my relations at home, I shall say nothing concerning them, as they have not for these six years past concerned themselves about me; excepting that I heartily wish them all well, and that my brothers and sisters may make a more prosperous voyage through this life than I have done.

Henry Vansittart, the Governor, to his great credit, was so amused by Martinett's will that he happily took on his share of responsibility and paid all his debts!

In 1965 a New York singing teacher died virtually penniless but still managed to file a will for probate leaving behind in cheerfulness and good nature what he lacked in goods and possessions:

(1) I direct that all my creditors be paid except my landlord.
(2) I give and bequeath to my good friend, Theodore Weber, my best aluminium tin if I die of anything but indigestion. In that event I give him a sad farewell.
(3) To my old friend, Ann Lewis, I give and bequeath Purcell's *Passing By*, which I wrongfully took and carried away last Christmas.
(4) I give and bequeath to my dear friend, Mrs George Hale, the satisfaction of being remembered in my will.
(5) To my old pal, Mary Ledgerwood, I give and bequeath the sum of 35 cents. It's not much but it's the beginning of a Scotch fortune.

(6) I leave to my lawyer, Huber Lewis, the task of explaining to my relatives why they didn't get a million dollars apiece.

(7) I appoint Huber Lewis executor of my will. In view of his profession, I suppose we had better require him to furnish a bond. I give him full power to sell, mortgage or pledge any or all of my estate for the purpose of paying the legacy left by Article 5, and if a sufficient sum cannot be realized, I warn him to be wary of the legatee.

The signatures of the three witnesses were preceded by his own version of a well-known Gilbert and Sullivan refrain:

Three little maids from school are we,
Called to witness this will, you see,
And testify to its propriety
Three little maids from school.
Everything has been properly done,
The testator's looks suggested a 'bun',
But he knew right enough we considered it fun,
Three little maids from school.

Other wills have left almost as little but have done so with a greater economy of words. A will filed for probate in New Jersey contained the one-line bequest:

To my wife Anna (who is no damn good) I leave $1.

In 1781, the last will and testament of John Aylett, hit out at an adversary in another way:

I hereby direct my executors to lay five guineas in purchase of a picture of a viper biting the benevolent hand of the person who saved him from perishing in the snow, if the same can be bought for the money; and that they do, in memory of me, present it to Edward Bearcroft, Esq., a King's Counsel, whereby he may have frequent opportunities for contemplating on it.

153

This I direct to be presented to him in lieu of a legacy of three thousand pounds which I had, by a former will, now revoked and burnt, left him.

A Philadelphia industrialist who died in 1947 made these bequests:

To my wife I leave her lover, and the knowledge that I wasn't the fool she thought I was.

To my son I leave the pleasure of earning a living. For twenty-five years he thought the pleasure was mine. He was mistaken.

To my daughter I leave $100,000. She will need it. The only piece of business her husband ever did was to marry her.

To may valet I leave the clothes he has been stealing from me for ten years. Also the fur coat he wore last summer while I was in Palm Beach.

To my chauffeur, I leave my cars. He almost ruined them and I want him to have the satisfaction of finishing the job.

To my partner, I leave the suggestion that he take some clever man in with him at once if he expects to do any business.

The fourth Earl of Pembroke died in 1650 and left one of the most entertaining aristocratic wills on record:

I, Philip, IV Earl of Pembroke and Montgomery, being, as I am assured, of unsound health, but of sound memory – as I well remember me that five years ago I did vote for the despatching of old Canterbury, neither have I forgotten that I did see my King upon the scaffold – yet as it is said that Death doth even now pursue me, and, moreover, as it is yet further said that it is my practice to yield under coercion, I do make my last will and testament.

Imprimis: As for my soul, I do confess I have often heard men speak of my soul, but what may be these same souls, or what their destination, God knoweth; for myself, I know not.

Men have likewise talked to me of another world, which I have never visited, nor do I even know an inch of the ground that leadeth thereto. When the King was reigning, I did make my son wear a surplice, being desirous that he should become a Bishop, and for myself I did follow the religion of my master; then came the Scotch, who made me a Presbyterian, but since the time of Cromwell, I have become an Independent. These are, methinks, the three principal religions of the Kingdom – if any of the three can save a soul, to that I claim to belong: if, therefore, my executors can find my soul, I desire they will return it to Him who gave it to me.

... put not my body beneath the church-porch for I am, after all, a man of birth, and I would not that I should be interred there, where Colonel Pride was born.

Item: I give my two best saddle-horses to the Earl of Denbigh whose legs, methinks, must soon begin to fail him. As regardeth my other horses, I bequeath them to Lord Fairfax, that when Cromwell and his council take away his commission he may still have some *horse* to command.

Item: I give nothing to my Lord Saye, and I do make him this legacy willingly, because I know that he will faithfully distribute it unto the poor.

Item: Seeing that I did menace a certain Henry Mildmay, but did not thrash him, I do leave the sum of fifty pounds sterling to the lacquey that shall pay unto him my debt.

Item: I bequeath to Thomas May, whose nose I did break at a mascarade, five shillings. My intention had been to give him more; but all who shall have seen his 'History of the Parliament' will consider that even this sum is too large.

Item: I give to the Lieutenant-General Cromwell one of my words, the which he must want, seeing that he hath never kept any of his own.

Item: I give up the ghost.

Anglo-Irish relations couldn't have been improved by the will of an Englishman living in Tipperary at the end of the eighteenth century, which left ten pounds to be paid annually in the following manner:

It is my will and pleasure that this sum shall be spent in the purchase of a certain quantity of liquor vulgarly called whiskey, and it shall be publicly given out that a certain number of persons, Irish only, not to exceed twenty, who may choose to assemble in the cemetery in which I shall be interred, on the anniversary of my death, shall have the same distributed to them. Further, it is my desire that each shall receive it by the half-a-pint at a time till the whole is consumed, each being likewise provided with a stout oaken stick and a knife, and that they shall drink it all on the spot.

Knowing what I know of the Irish character, my conviction is, that with these materials given they will not fail to destroy each other, and when in the course of time the race comes to be exterminated, this neighbourhood at least may, perhaps, be colonized by civilized and respected Englishmen.

Wills with a sting in the tail have been popular with testators for hundreds of years. Many have tried to carry out through their wills what they singularly failed to achieve during their lives. Here's Lord Chesterfield leaving the bulk of his fortune to his godson, Philip Stanhope, and making sure that his inheritance lasted longer than it might otherwise have done:

... in case my said godson Philip Stanhope shall at any time hereafter keep, or be concerned in the keeping of, any racehorse or racehorses, or pack or packs of hounds, or reside one night in Newmarket, that infamous seminary of iniquity and ill-manners during the course of the races there, or shall resort to the said races, or shall use in any one day at any game or bet whatsoever the sum of £500, then, and in any of the cases aforesaid, it is my express Will, that he my said Godson shall forfeit and pay out of my estate the sum of £5,000 to and for the use of the Dean and Chapter of Westminster, for every such offence or misdemeanour as is above specified, to be recovered by action for debt in any of his Majesty's Courts of Record at Westminster.

Death where is thy sting?

The daughter of a Yorkshire vicar was left a considerable sum in her father's will on the condition that she modified her wardrobe. As the will states:

> Seeing that my daughter Anna has not availed herself of my advice touching the objectionable practice of going about with her arms bare up to the elbows, my will is that, should she continue after my death this violation of the modesty of her sex, all the goods, chattels, moneys, land, and other that I have sevised to her for the maintenance of her future life shall pass to the oldest of the sons of my sister Caroline.
>
> Should anyone take exception to this my wish as being too severe, I answer that license in dress in a woman is a mark of a depraved mind.

When Henry Durrell died in 1924 his will revealed that he couldn't decide to which of his nephews he should leave his estate. In the end he decided luck should settle what he had failed to do. The three young men had to throw dice for the fortune!

The secret ambitions of a wealthy Argentinian were revealed in his 1955 will, in which part of his immense fortune was left to the Teatro Dramatico in Buenos Aires. Juan Potomachi explained this bequest as follows:

> All my life I wanted to be on the stage. Lack of talent prevented me at first from realizing that wish. Later my position in the community as a prominent business man barred me altogether from the stage.
>
> I leave 200,000 pesos to a fund from which talented young actors shall get yearly scholarships. My only condition is that my head be preserved and used as the skull in *Hamlet*.
>
> My dearest wish would be thereby fulfilled after all, as I would still have a part in a play after my death.

Mrs Frederica Cook made her mark on posterity with a will drawn up at the beginning of this century which filled four bound volumes and consisted of 95,940 words!

The First Division of the Court of Session in Edinburgh were faced with an unusual problem when presented with the will of the founder of a chain of well-known hotels. In his generosity the testator had left a bequest of £6,000 for the benefit of teetotal tailors in 'necessitous circumstances'.

The will of William Hickington, proved in York in 1770, reads:

I, William Hickington,
Poet of Pocklington,
Do give and bequeath,
As free as I breathe,
To thee, Mary Jarum,
Queen of my Harum,
My cash and my cattle,
With every chattel,
To have and to hold
Come heat or come cold,
Sans hindrance or strife,
Though thou art not my wife.
As witness my hand,
Just here as I stand,
The twelfth of July,
In the year Seventy.

Entertaining as many of these wills are, I suppose we ought in the end to spare a thought for the lawyers and judges who have the frequently unenviable task of executing the conditions of the more eccentric testators. Mr Justice Eve spoke for all of them when he commented:

I shudder to think that in the hereafter I shall have to meet those testators whose wishes on earth have been frustrated by my judgements.

In 1880 a tailor in New York died leaving a will that stipulated:

I own seventy-one pairs of trousers, and I strictly enjoin my executors to hold a public sale at which these shall be sold to the highest bidder, and the proceeds distributed to the poor of the city.

I desire that these garments shall in no way be examined or meddled with, but be disposed of as are found at the time of my death; and no purchaser to buy more than one pair.

This last paragraph turned out to have greater significance than the deceased's executors or relatives might have imagined. The sale was duly held and the city's needy bid for the second-hand trousers. All found the pockets sewn up. All opened them. And all found a thousand dollars in bank notes hidden inside!

Non-fiction

☐	**The Money Book**	Margaret Allen	£2.95p
☐	**Fall of Fortresses**	Elmer Bendiner	£1.75p
☐	**The British Way of Birth**	Catherine Boyd and Lea Sellers	£1.50p
☐	**100 Great British Weekends**	John Carter	£2.95p
☐	**Last Waltz in Vienna**	George Clare	£1.95p
☐	**Walker's Britain**	Andrew Duncan	£4.95p
☐	**Travellers' Britain**	Arthur Eperon	£2.95p
☐	**The Tropical Traveller**	John Hatt	£2.50p
☐	**The Lord God Made Them All**	James Herriot	£1.95p
☐	**The Neck of the Giraffe**	Francis Hitching	£2.50p
☐	**A Small Town is a World**	David Kossoff	£1.00p
☐	**Prayers and Graces**	Allen Laing illus. by Mervyn Peake	£1.25p
☐	**Kitchen & Bathroom Book**	Jose Manser	£5.95p
☐	**Best of Shrdlu**	Denys Parsons	£1.00p
☐	**Dipped in Vitriol**	Nicholas Parsons	£1.75p
☐	**The Bargain Book**	Barty Phillips	£1.95p
☐	**Thy Neighbour's Wife**	Gay Talese	£1.75p
☐	**Just off for the Weekend**	John Slater	£2.50p
☐	**Dead Funny**	Fritz Spiegl	£1.50p
☐	**The Third Wave**	Alvin Toffler	£2.75p
☐	**The World Atlas of Treasure**	Derek Wilson	£6.50p
☐	**Shyness**	Philip Zimbardo	£1.95p

All these books are available at your local bookshop or newsagent, or can be ordered direct from the publisher. Indicate the number of copies required and fill in the form below   10

....

Name_____

(Block letters please)

Address_____

_____

Send to CS Department, Pan Books Ltd, PO Box 40, Basingstoke, Hants
Please enclose remittance to the value of the cover price plus:
35p for the first book plus 15p per copy for each additional book ordered
to a maximum charge of £1.25 to cover postage and packing
Applicable only in the UK

While every effort is made to keep prices low, it is sometimes necessary to increase prices at short notice. Pan Books reserve the right to show on covers and charge new retail prices which may differ from those advertised in the text or elsewhere